WISDOM OF THE WORD

Bible Study Series

I0901141

Acts

The Church Ignited

Part 2

Dee Kelley

Jeannie McCullough, Executive Editor

BEACON HILL PRESS
OF KANSAS CITY

ISBN-13: 978-0-8341-2282-6
ISBN-10: 0-8341-2282-0
Printed in the United States of America

Cover Design: Darlene Filley

Library of Congress Cataloging-in-Publication Data

Kelley, Dee, 1956-
Acts : the church ignited / Dee Kelley.
p. cm. — (Wisdom of the word bible study series)
Includes bibliographical references.
ISBN-13: 978-0-8341-2281-9 (pt. 1 : pbk.)
ISBN-10: 0-8341-2281-2 (pt. 1 : pbk.)
ISBN-13: 978-0-8341-2282-6 (pt. 2 : pbk.)
ISBN-10: 0-8341-2282-0 (pt. 2 : pbk.)
1. Bible. N.T. Acts—Textbooks. I. Title.

BS2626.K45 2006
226.60071—dc22

2006025964

10 9 8 7 6 5 4 3 2 1

Contents

About Wisdom of the Word

Wisdom of the Word (W.O.W.) was founded in 1986 by Jeannie McCullough in Bethany, Oklahoma. It began as a weekly Bible study at Bethany First Church of the Nazarene. In the first year the study grew to over 400 members, and women from other churches and the community began joining. The local enrollment of Wisdom of the Word eventually exceeded 1,000 and has included men, women, and children of all ages and many denominations.

Wisdom of the Word has been an instrument in uniting the community of believers as well as reaching the unchurched and the lost. It is now ministering to thousands through videos and cassette tapes and other programs such as Children of the Word, prison ministries, and missions.

About the Name

W.O.W. began as "Women of the Word." Then when men began to join in the study with the women, the name was changed to "Wisdom of the Word," not only to retain the W.O.W. acronym but also to reflect the mission: to have our lives visibly changed by gaining wisdom from God's Word and responding in radical obedience to His voice.

About Jeannie McCullough

Jeannie McCullough was a pastor's wife until June 2004. She is also a mother and grandmother. Her life and ministry have taken her to Bethany, Oklahoma, where her husband, Mel, served as senior pastor of Bethany First Church of the Nazarene. In June 2004 he accepted the position of inaugural president of the Nazarene Foundation, located in Olathe, Kansas, near Kansas City. Since that time they have been in transition between Oklahoma City and Kansas City. Jeannie understands firsthand how radical obedience to God's Word can change a life.

Southern Nazarene University granted Jeannie an honorary doctorate in 1997. Due to her humor and honesty as well as her unique insights and application of the Scriptures in daily living, she is in great demand as a speaker throughout North America. Jeannie strives to be a "salt tablet" who will make others thirst for God's Word. As she has committed herself to being a student of the Word, God has given her many opportunities to share what He is teaching her.

About the Author

DEE KELLEY is pastor of First Church of the Nazarene in San Diego. He is a popular youth speaker and has served as dean of student development at Mount Vernon Nazarene University and Olivet Nazarene University. Most recently he served as vice president of spiritual development at Southern Nazarene University, overseeing chapel services, missions, and small-group ministries on the campus. He and his wife, Kay, live in San Diego with their two daughters, Sutton and Savannah.

Introduction to Acts

Often we turn on the news and see images of ravaging wildfires. Firefighters from across the country are brought in to combat fires that seem out of control. Acres upon acres are consumed by the flames. Specialists arrive at the scene to determine the origin of the fire. Their findings frequently point to something as simple as a spark from a campfire, a match, or a firecracker. We are truly amazed that something with such small beginnings could produce such enormous power and so radically change everything it touches.

Nearly 2,000 years ago a match was struck in Palestine. Following Jesus' resurrection, He appeared to His followers for a period of 40 days (Acts 1:3). Shortly before His final ascension into heaven, Jesus instructed them to stay in Jerusalem and wait for the gift of the Father. This gift was the Holy Spirit, a heavenly spark that ignited the hearts of the followers who had gathered as Jesus had instructed. The flames immediately spread beyond that room and became a raging fire of grace destined to consume the lives of men and women around the world. The small beginnings in an upper room in Palestine released an enormous power that continues to radically change everything it touches.

The Book of Acts provides an account of the Holy Spirit "flame" and the fire it ignited. It is a historical account of the birth of the Christian Church and the spread of the gospel message. Although the Scriptures do not specifically say so, we believe Luke to be the author. In Paul's letter to the Colossians, he refers to Luke as the "beloved physician." This medical doctor and historian was highly concerned with accurately conveying the details reported by those who were eyewitnesses of the events about which he writes.

Acts is the second of two books written by Dr. Luke. The first book, the Gospel according to Luke, covers the life of Jesus. The book spans the 30 years prior to and including the resurrection of Jesus. The Book of Acts covers the 30 years following the Resurrection. It is the first Church history book ever written. Acts is the story of how the Church began and how the early believers spread the good news of Jesus. The apostle Peter is the dominant character for the first 12 chapters of the book, while Paul takes center stage for the remaining 16 chapters.

Luke does not mention any specific dates in his writings, though he does make reference to political facts, the dates of which we know from other historians. The book concludes during the second year of Paul's imprisonment. This means that it could not have been completed before A.D. 62. We also know of several very significant events that happened between A.D. 64 and A.D. 70 that the Book of Acts does not mention. Therefore, we conclude that it was completed prior to A.D. 64.

In this study of Acts we want you to experience an exciting, enlightening, and empowering journey as we watch the first flaming witnesses tell their world that Jesus is alive. We will watch as they witness to their personal knowledge of the resurrected Christ and of His transforming power. Our Counselor for this study was present for all the events recorded in the book. He is *the true light that gives light to every man* (John 1:9). Allow Him to light a flame in you. Let these small beginnings release the enormous power of the Holy Spirit so that you might be transformed into His likeness.

As you begin each day, use this acrostic to help you study:

***W**ait for the Holy Spirit to teach you as you read His Word.*

***O**bey what God instructs you to do.*

***R**emember to praise God for insights and promises fulfilled.*

***D**iscover for yourself the incredible faithfulness of God!*

Acts

■ A Study of Acts 13

LESSON 11

DAY ONE

Work as Worship

Read Acts 13, focusing on verses 1-3.

1. Who was set apart? (See verse 2.)

2. For what purpose were they set apart? (See verse 2.)

All around us we see the beauty of God's creation. We are the beneficiaries of His work. The apostle John says that all things were created through the word of God. Then the Word became flesh and lived among us (John 1:14), and they called His name Jesus.

Jesus was not exempt from work during His time on earth. He certainly had chores as a boy, learned a trade as a young man, and likely applied that trade at some point in His adult life. He had to grow, learn, work, and do the common things that are part of all of our lives from birth to adulthood.

In the days in which Jesus lived, Jewish fathers taught their sons a trade. Jesus' father was a carpenter. Under His father's tutelage, Jesus likely experienced the joy of cutting his first board and the frustration of making a corner joint. He knew firsthand the difficulties and satisfaction of a good day's work. The carpenter's shop was a place where He could learn the trade of His earthly father and the wisdom of His Heavenly Father.

3. Luke summarizes the early years of Jesus' life in Luke 2:52. Write the verse below.

This verse provides only a small glimpse into these years of Jesus' life but enough to discover that before His public ministry began, His life and work made a positive impact on people. In John 5:17 Jesus said, *My Father is always at his work to this very day, and I, too, am working.* Through Jesus we see the nature of the Father. God created the world and then rested, but He did not quit working. He is still at work, and He offers His followers the incredible privilege of joining Him in His work. In fact, the Word says that we are *God's fellow workers* (2 Corinthians 6:1).

4. Look up 2 Corinthians 5:20, and record below one of the ways in which we work with God.

Some of us are not only responsible for our own work, but we also have responsibility over the work of others. Leaders must handle that responsibility with wisdom and compassion. For those in this position, there is even a great need to unite work with worship. Through the prophet Isaiah, God expressed His anger toward those who had separated the two.

5. Read Isaiah 58:3-8.
   a. According to verses 3-4, what were the people accused of doing on the day of fasting?

MEMORY CHALLENGE

Psalm 63:7

Because you are my help, I will sing in the shadow of your wings.

b. Using verses 6-7, list the things that describe the kind of fast God has chosen.

6. We are told in Acts 13 that many in the church at Antioch were using their gifts for the work of the Kingdom. Some are described as prophets and teachers. Five of these individuals are mentioned by name. List them below.

a. How is Barnabas described in Acts 11:24?

b. Some think that Simeon may have been the same man mentioned in Mark 15:21. If it is the same man, what does that verse say he did?

c. Lucius is probably one of the men mentioned in Acts 11:20. If that is true, what had he been doing?

d. Manaen was a "foster brother" to Herod. They were raised together in the palace court. They played, laughed, and studied together. However, as adults they had very little in common. The personal choices they made took them in different directions. Manaen became a prophet or teacher of the gospel. Look up Matthew 14:6-11. What would you say Herod became?

e. Read Acts 9:27-28. What are Saul's characteristics?

7. Have you ever felt that God has called you to do a "special assignment"? If you are willing, share that assignment with your group.

8. How does God's work coincide with your vocational work?

DAY TWO

Double Blind

Read Acts 13:1-12.

1. According to verses 1-3, who sent Saul and Barnabas off?

2. According to verse 4, who sent Saul and Barnabas on their way?

3. What do we learn about the way the Church functions in relationship to the Holy Spirit?

The Church is blind without the guidance of the Holy Spirit. It wanders aimlessly, accomplishing little, unless its actions are Spirit-led. After the church at Antioch had worshiped and fasted, the Holy Spirit gave them direction. They continued to fast and pray as they followed the Spirit's leading. Many of us seek God's leadership before a decision is made but fail to continue that process after the decision has been made. One lesson we can learn from this early group of believers is that it is important to seek God's direction both before and after a decision has been made. Sensing God's direction is not the end of the process but rather the beginning.

After praying and fasting, Simeon, Lucius, and Manaen (and possibly others of the church at the Antioch) laid their hands on Barnabas and Saul, identifying with them as their Spirit-chosen substitutes, and sent them on their way. The two of them were joined by John Mark.

4. The home of John Mark's mother was a place where the early Christians gathered. According to Acts 12:12, what was one of the activities of the believers when they gathered at her home?

The three sojourners—Barnabas, Saul, and John Mark—left Antioch and walked about 16 miles to Seleucia, the port city of Antioch, where they boarded a ship sailing for Cyprus, Barnabas's home. They landed at Salamis, the commercial capital of the island, and preached God's Word. They went first to the synagogues, to their own people who had some knowledge of biblical things. There they preached the Good News.

The trio traveled the length of the island from Salamis to Paphos, the political capital. Here they met a Jew named Bar-Jesus (also known as Elymas), who was not only a sorcerer but also a false prophet. Elymas apparently had no reverence for the Old Testament scriptures, because God commanded Jews to have nothing to do with divination or sorcery (Deuteronomy 18:10-12). He was the attendant to Sergius Paulus, the proconsul governor. But Sergius Paulus wanted to hear the Word of God from Barnabas and Saul and sent for them. Elymas tried to prevent his boss from accepting the faith. However, Elymas overestimated his own influence, underestimated the courage of Saul, and discounted the power of God's Spirit to intervene.

Elymas was blind to the truth of God. His tricks and sorcery had left him in spiritual darkness. Saul might have recognized himself in Elymas. It had not been very long since Saul had been *breathing out murderous threats against the Lord's disciples* (Acts 9:1). The Lord struck Saul blind and through that process called him to be a chosen instrument to carry the name of the Lord before Gentiles, their kings, and the people of Israel (Acts 9:15). Here in Acts 13, Sergius Paulus became Paul's first recorded Gentile convert. At the same time, Saul proclaimed God's judgment of blindness on Elymas. The outward condition of Elymas now matched his inward futility.

Our outward talents and blessings can often prevent us from seeing our inward poverty. When those outward gifts are taken away, we might call it a tragedy. However, if it causes us to confront our emptiness and leads us to God's truth, then what was perceived as a tragedy could be the greatest blessing of all. We do not know how the story ends for Elymas, but we can hope that his blindness did for him what it did for Saul.

5. Read 2 Kings 6:8-23.
   a. Who was healed of blindness in verse 17?

   b. Who was blinded in verse 18?

   c. Based on what you read in verses 22-23, what was Elisha's intent in asking God to blind the men?

6. Read 2 Peter 1:5-9. When can a follower of God be spiritually blind?

7. Explain what you think Jesus means in John 9:39.

8. Give an example of when God has healed a "blind spot" in your spiritual journey.

MEMORY CHALLENGE

Why do we sing?

DAY THREE

History Lesson

Read Acts 13:13-25.

Paphos was a port city on the west end of the island of Cyprus. It is still a beautiful small harbor town today, but back then it was also a political center for the island. Paul and the others sailed northwest, back to the mainland, to the city of Perga. There John Mark left them and went back to Jerusalem. Based on this passage, we might think that he went back to Jerusalem to report the good things that happened on Cyprus. However, there is another passage of Scripture that indicates the fact that his departure was not so positive.

1. Read Acts 15:36-38. How is John Mark's departure described?

This incident became part of John Mark's history. It was not an event that would define his character but was nevertheless a part of his history. God does not ignore our history or erase our history. Instead, it is often through history that God brings redemption. We will read more about John Mark later in Acts. However, this passage contains another history lesson regarding God's redemptive work.

On the Sabbath day Paul and Barnabas went to the synagogue. They sat down and listened to the reading of the Law and the Prophets. Following the reading, the synagogue rulers asked if Paul and Barnabas had a message of encouragement. This was all Paul needed. He was on his feet and began to lay the foundation for telling the people the Good News, reciting some of the history of God's dealings with Israel. This was probably a familiar speaking style to the audience. Peter and Stephen used this approach, and so did Paul. He wove together the centuries of history to point the audience toward Jesus, the Messiah.

2. Paul made reference to several specific events out of Israel's history. Match his statements to the appropriate Scripture reference. (If it would help you, write a one-word description by the Acts scripture.)

Acts 13:17	2 Samuel 5:3
Acts 13:18	Joshua 12:7-24
Acts 13:19	1 Samuel 8:4-5
Acts 13:20	Matthew 3:1-2
Acts 13:21	Exodus 1:6-7
Acts 13:22	Luke 3:16
Acts 13:23	Joshua 5:6-7
Acts 13:24	1 Samuel 3:10-11
Acts 13:25	Matthew 1:6-16

Paul's audience would have been very familiar with the events to which Paul referred. Their faith was tied up in their history. Their confidence in God's redemption in the future was based on their observation of His protection and guidance in the past. Paul showed them how God, through Jesus, had stepped into history and provided redemption for all.

3. To whom did Paul address his comments? (See Acts 13:16.)

4. What did God promise? (See verse 23.)

5. What was the historical setting when Jesus first entered your life?

6. Can you describe a part of your history (such as difficult events or circumstances) that God has redeemed (used for His glory and your growth)?

MEMORY CHALLENGE

Look up the memory verse, and read it in the context of the verses that surround it.

DAY FOUR

The Puzzle Pieces

Read Acts 13:26-31.

1. Who did not recognize Jesus? (See verse 27.)

2. What did the rulers and people of Jerusalem inadvertently do when they condemned and executed Jesus? (See verses 27 and 29.)

3. Match the prophecies from only one psalm (Psalm 22) to the events of Jesus' life.

Psalm 22:1	Matthew 27:39
Psalm 22:7	Matthew 27:43
Psalm 22:8	Matthew 27:46
Psalm 22:14	Mark 15:25
Psalm 22:15	Luke 23:34
Psalm 22:16	John 19:28
Psalm 22:17	John 19:33
Psalm 22:18	John 19:34

Once when I was a child I was given a very simple puzzle consisting of two thick nails, each of which was bent into a loop. The two looped nails were connected to one another with the loop of the first nail interlocked with the loop of the second nail. The object was to separate the two nails. The puzzle looked simple, but the more I tried the more frustrated I became. I soon came to the conclusion that the nails had been bent into their current configuration and that, without bending the nails again, it was impossible to separate them. I handed them back, and within seconds my friend had the two nails separated. He then asked me to put them back together. I could not do that either. I was looking at the same two puzzle pieces he was looking at, but I could not make the connection. Finally, he showed me the proper angle that allowed the nails to slide into an interlocking connection and slide back out again. Once I learned how to separate the nails, it was simple. I have never forgotten the solution.

In a similar fashion, the people in Paul's audience had the puzzle pieces given them by the prophets. Paul lays out the puzzle pieces and explains that the "solution" for which they have been looking is Jesus, the Messiah. This is truly good news. They had probably heard of Jesus, but on this day they heard a man, an obvious scholar and a trained rabbi, convincingly declare that Jesus was the long-awaited Christ. The puzzle pieces had all been there. Now the pieces came together.

4. According to Acts 13:26, who was in Paul's audience?

5. To whom was the message of salvation sent? (See verse 26.)

6. Who saw Jesus after His resurrection? (See verse 31.)

7. What were they doing on behalf of Jesus? (See verse 31).

8. How has Jesus been an answer to some of the puzzle pieces in your life?

MEMORY CHALLENGE

Write what you think the memory verse meant to the first people who heard it or read it.

DAY FIVE

God's Great Gift

Read Acts 13:32-43.

1. In Acts 13:36-37, what distinction did Paul draw between King David and Jesus?

2. What is the good news? (See verses 32-33.)

3. Find the story of the Resurrection in each of the four Gospels (Matthew, Mark, Luke, and John). Record the chapter references below.

4. What is proclaimed through Jesus? (See verse 38.)

5. Read the following verses about forgiveness, and summarize them in your own words.

Acts 10:43

Ephesians 1:7

Colossians 1:13-14

1 John 1:9

6. As we learned yesterday, the Old Testament writers had foretold the coming of the Messiah. The apostle Peter tells us that the prophets searched intently to try to determine the time and circumstances in which the Messiah would come, suffer, and then be glorified. Read 1 Peter 1:10-12. The beginning of verse 12 tells whom the prophets were serving when they spoke of Christ. What was their conclusion?

Both the prophets Micah and Isaiah spoke of a person who would announce the coming of the Messiah. John the Baptist was that man. Before Herod beheaded him, John emphatically declared that he was the herald of the coming King, that his ministry was to announce and introduce the Messiah. His words fanned a flame of hope for all Jews, in Israel and abroad, that God would soon reveal the promised One. John was highly regarded by most Jews, and Paul used John's credibility to confirm his own declarations about Jesus. The Messiah had come. Furthermore, He had come for the benefit of both the Jews and Gentiles.

The Gentiles were particularly attracted to Paul's message, which made no distinction between Jew and Gentile. They had learned about the law, but forgiveness through faith in Jesus was better than the law. The law could not justify guilty people. It could corner them, convict them and condemn them, but it could never cancel their sin. It could cover sin but never remove it. According to Paul, what God's law could not do had now been done through God's Son, Jesus. His listeners were stunned and sobered by what they heard. They wanted to hear more, so they invited Paul and Barnabas to come back the next Sabbath day.

7. The good news is that the Messiah has come and has provided a way of salvation for everyone. What the law could not do Jesus did by His life, death, and resurrection. Paul explains this amazing truth in greater detail in his letter to the Romans. Three simple verses taken from that letter explain God's great gift. Write these verses that follow:

Romans 3:23

Romans 6:23

Romans 10:9

Pray a prayer of confession or a prayer of thanksgiving, or both.

MEMORY CHALLENGE

When you are away from the house, call home and leave the memory verse on your answering machine. Check yourself for accuracy when you get home.

DAY SIX

Joy in My Heart

Read Acts 13:44-52.

1. Who showed up on the Sabbath? (See verse 44.)

2. What had they come to hear? (See verse 44.)

3. What caused the Jews to talk abusively against what Paul was saying? (See Acts 13:45.)

4. Why did Paul and Barnabas turn to the Gentiles? (See verses 46-47.)

5. Whom did the Jews incite to stir up persecution against Paul and Barnabas?

6. According to Acts 13:52, were the disciples discouraged? How are they described?

7. As a result of the time spent in Syrian Antioch, what happened to the Word of the Lord? (See verse 49.)

Word quickly spread throughout the city concerning Paul and Barnabas. The city was comprised of both Jews and Gentiles. Both groups were interested in what they might see and hear from the two visitors. However, the Jews had a different reaction than the Gentiles when they saw the large crowds—they were filled with jealousy. We do not know if they thought their power was being threatened or their authority was being undermined, or if they were simply upset that the visitors were getting more attention than they were.

Jealousy can be a silent killer. Much like resentment (or a spirit of unforgiveness), it usually does more harm to the person who harbors such feelings than it ever does to the object of the jealousy. It can rob a person of spiritual vitality, destroy relationships, and produce vicious language. Jealousy presumes to know the motivation or thoughts of another person, assumes an attitude of self-righteousness, and ceases to believe that God is in control.

The jealousy of the Jews produced abusive language. They spoke against what Paul was saying. They rejected the good news and incited others to do the same. Their jealousy burned so hot that they were not satisfied with simply rejecting the words of Paul and Barnabas—they had to physically reject them as well. They stirred up persecution against the two and had them thrown out of the region. Jealousy is never fully satiated, just temporarily appeased. The only antidote is confession, forgiveness, and renewal. Ironically, the Jews had rejected the very thing that could forgive their sin and heal their jealous hearts.

In contrast to the Jews, the Gentiles received the truth and were filled with joy (verse 52). When I was a kid, my dad led music at our church. Every once in a while he would lead us in this Sunday School chorus:

I have the joy, joy, joy, joy down in my heart.
Where? Down in my heart.
Where? Down in my heart.
I have the joy, joy, joy, joy down in my heart.
Where? Down in my heart to stay.

He would add other verses, like "I have the Sunday School enthusiasm down in my heart" or "I have the peace that passeth understanding down in my heart." But I have always loved the original verse, because it perfectly describes the feeling that accompanies the receiving of the good news of Jesus Christ. Maybe the Gentiles sang a similar song when the truth of Paul's words gripped their lives.

MEMORY CHALLENGE

Find some way to use the Memory Challenge in a conversation today.

Acts

■ A Study of Acts 14

LESSON 12

DAY ONE

Dusty Feet

Read Acts 13:49—14:7.

1. Where did Paul and Barnabas go after leaving Pisidian Antioch? (See verse 14:1.)

2. Who enabled Paul and Barnabas to do miraculous signs and wonders? (See verse 3.)

3. With what were the disciples who remained in Pisidian Antioch filled? (See Acts 13:52.)

Paul and Barnabas were "expelled" from Antioch, but believers were not discouraged by this turn of events. They moved on to Iconium, and the Lord went with them —but He also remained to nurture and keep the new converts.

Before His death and resurrection, Jesus was limited in both time and space. He could be in only one place at one time. When He ascended to heaven and poured out His Spirit on His obedient followers, those restrictions were removed. He could simultaneously be with the persecuted saints in Jerusalem, His missionaries on their way to Iconium, and with believers everywhere. Through the power and presence of the Holy Spirit, the Lord is present with every believer at all times. Paul and Barnabas left the new believers in Pisidian Antioch, but the Holy Spirit remained.

As Paul and Barnabas traveled the 80 or 90 miles to Iconium, they probably reviewed what had happened in the town they had just left, and they planned for what might occur in the town they were about to enter. No doubt they rejoiced over the changed lives they had seen but also felt remorse for the ones who still denied Jesus as the Messiah. They were not alone as they walked. Jesus had promised that the Holy Spirit would be with them and would counsel them. The future would bring more difficulties, even life-threatening situations. Paul and Barnabas had already been transformed by the things the Holy Spirit had taught them, but there was more to learn.

4. What was the last act of Paul and Barnabas as they left Pisidian Antioch? (See 13:51.)

5. For what situation did Jesus instruct His disciples to do the same? (See Matthew 10:14.)

The disciples' gesture was a significant act. The Jews would often shake the dust off their feet when they would return to their homeland from another country. The purpose was to remove anything that might defile their sacred land. The disciples used this act in a similar way. First, it

MEMORY CHALLENGE

Ephesians 4:29

Do not let any unwholesome talk come out of your mouths, but only what is helpful for building others up according to their needs, that it may benefit those who listen.

served as a reminder to themselves that the grace of God is sacred. They should never allow the rebuff, persecution, or animosity of others to defile the "sacred ground" of their new life in Christ. Symbolically shaking off those things that cloud the message of grace keeps the bad influences from robbing our inheritance of joy.

Second, the act of shaking off the dust served as a warning to others, or as scripture describes it, as a "protest." The act essentially said that the people of Pisidian Antioch were worse than heathens. Heathens have not yet heard the Good News. These people had heard the Good News and yet had rejected it. In shaking the dust off their feet, Paul and Barnabas were saying that the people were on dangerous ground.[1] The Holy Spirit was convicting them of sin but was also offering forgiveness and new life. Those who rejected Paul and Barnabas were also rejecting the Holy Spirit. That rejection has eternal consequences. When the Holy Spirit moves in your life, listen and obey.

6. *a.* How long did Paul and Barnabas stay in Iconium? (See verse 3.)

   b. Were they timid in their witness concerning Jesus? Support your answer using scripture.

   c. How did the Lord assist them in convincing the Jewish nonbelievers? (See verse 3.)

7. Read John 14:15-17. Who will be with us forever?

8. Read John 14:26. What will the Holy Spirit do?

9. Read John 16:7-8. What else will the Counselor, God's Spirit, do?

Has the Holy Spirit convicted you of anything that you should "shake off your feet"? Listen to His leading.

DAY TWO

Crippled Feet

Read Acts 14:8-10.

1. In the town of Lystra lived a crippled man. How long had he been crippled? (See verse 8.)

2. What did Paul see in him? (See verse 9.)

3. In response to Paul's word, what did the man do? (See verse 10.)

4. We studied a similar miracle in Lesson 3. Read Acts 3:1-8. List some of the similarities in the two stories.

In Scripture we can often find a spiritual parallel to a physical healing. Here, in Lystra, Paul healed a man who was crippled. He had no ability to stand on his own. In the same way, Paul had been preaching and teaching to people who were spiritually crippled. In Iconium and Antioch, as well as Lystra, there were some who had the faith to be healed and others who did not.

Paul spoke the truth with clarity and power. He gave his listeners the opportunity to accept or reject Jesus Christ. Before one can accept Christ, he or she must be willing to admit need for Christ. This man knew he was crippled and had the faith to be healed. Many of us are too proud to admit we are crippled by life's circumstances, by the actions of others, or by our own choices. Because of our human tendency to rebel against God, we have truly been crippled from birth. Admitting the need and believing on Christ give us the faith to begin to walk again.

A member of my family has high cholesterol. If unchecked, this problem can have fatal consequences. Until a few years ago, he did not know he had a problem. He was not overweight, did not lead a sedentary lifestyle, and ate few fatty foods. He discovered the problem when he went in for a general physical examination. At that point he had a choice: to admit the problem and get help or ignore the problem and pretend it did not exist. In the same way, the Holy Spirit points out the "crippled" areas of our life. He admonishes us to let the healing begin.

5. Read John 12:42-43. Based on this passage, why do many not confess their faith and consequently do not receive the Holy Spirit's help?

6. Read Romans 1:28. What happens to those who choose not to retain the knowledge of God?

7. Read Romans 8:5-6. What happens when you give control to the Holy Spirit?

8. Is there an area of your life that God has healed or is healing? Is there an area that is crippled that needs His touch? If you are willing, write them below and share them with your group.

MEMORY CHALLENGE

Read the memory verse aloud five times.

DAY THREE

Mistaken Feet

Read Acts 14:11-18.

1. What did the crowds shout when they saw what Paul had done? (See verse 11.)

2. What names did they give to Paul and Barnabas? (See verse 12.)

The actions of the people may not seem so strange if we understand the history of that region of the world. At the time Acts was written, many towns and cities had a mythological god that the people believed protected them. Zeus was the patron god of Lystra. The province of Lycaonia included the city of Lystra. This area was named for a myth that depicted Zeus as having once visited the province in human form. The people had long anticipated the return of Zeus and his eloquent companion Hermes.[1]

Paul and Barnabas fit the image of the gods these people worshiped. Paul was eloquent and the chief spokesperson. This was a characteristic of Zeus's messenger, Hermes. Barnabas was likely larger than Paul and must have had characteristics that matched their image of Zeus. One of the city's most influential citizens, the priest of Zeus, ratified these opinions by bringing animals to sacrifice to Paul and Barnabas. This sequence of events shows how truth is not always hindered by outright denial, but rather it is hindered by the filters or biases through which the truth is received.

The mistaken identify of Paul and Barnabas gave the two of them instant credibility and notoriety. They were immediately catapulted into a position of power. They could have used this mistaken identity to their personal advantage. The people were ready to worship them. Paul and Barnabas, however, were horrified. They ran into the crowd shouting, "we too are only men, human like you" (verse 15). Their hearts had been cleansed by the presence of the Lord; therefore they simply wanted the people to worship the one and only God. To worship another would be blasphemy.

God gave this commandment: *You shall have no other gods besides me* (Deuteronomy 5:7). This story shows how misdirected praise can become a violation of God's law. In regard to the people of the city, the praise that belonged to Jehovah God was being given to Zeus and Hermes. From the perspective of Paul and Barnabas, the praise that belonged to Jehovah God was being given to the two of them. It is unlikely that anyone of us will ever be mistaken for Zeus. However, we will all probably be in a position in which we receive praise that should be redirected to Jehovah God. Mistaken identity occurs when people's praise and worship are directed toward other people rather than God. We must be only a sign that points people toward the One who is truly worthy of praise.

3. Read Matthew 4:8-10.

   a. How did Jesus respond when tempted with power?

   b. What was Satan's desire for himself?

4. What do you think Jesus meant by His words in John 5:41?

5. Read John 12:42-43. What is the difference between the people in this passage, and Paul and Barnabas?

6. What does Paul say about himself in Galatians 1:10?

7. The people of Lystra were biased in the way they viewed divine matters. What are some of the prejudices or misconceptions you held regarding God before you became a Christian or as a young Christian?

8. What are the false ideas some of your unbelieving acquaintances have about the Christian faith?

9. List some ways in which our actions (the way in which we live out our faith) can help dispel false notions of Christianity and false ideas about God.

MEMORY CHALLENGE

Ask a friend or family member to listen as you recite the Memory Challenge.

DAY FOUR

Healed Feet

Read Acts 14:19-20.

1. Who turned the crowd against Paul and Barnabas? (See verse 19.)

2. What did the crowd do to Paul? (See verse 19.)

3. Acts 7:57-58 is the conclusion of the story of Stephen. Read the passage. Who was the young man who watched the coats?

4. Is there any difference between what the crowds did to Stephen in Acts 7:58 and what they did to Paul in Acts 14:19? If so, what is the difference?

5. Stoning was a form of capital punishment established by Old Testament law. Read Leviticus 24:15-16.

   a. What is the sin punishable by stoning?

   b. Read verse 14. Where is the stoning supposed to take place?

The Jews from Antioch and Iconium turned the responsive crowd into a frenzied mob. Their anger was evident in that they did not wait to take Paul outside the city before the stoning began. Instead, they stoned him and then dragged him out of the city. One of the reasons the punishment was to be taken outside the city limits was to allow time and opportunity for those who might want to speak on behalf of the accused to do so.[1] This angry crowd did not want reason, argument, or explanation. They wanted revenge. And so the stoning took place within the city. How often do our quick judgments, jealousy, and resentment prevent us from hearing an explanation or all the facts? How often do we "stone" another person's reputation without waiting for the truth to be fully heard?

Paul's feet and legs buckled beneath him. He collapsed under the onslaught of the stones. He appeared dead (and maybe actually was dead) and was dragged out of the city. The disciples followed, and when the angry crowd dissipated, they gathered around him. Life returned to his heart. Strength returned to his feet and legs. He stood up and walked back into the city.

As all this was happening, did Paul remember Stephen? Did he remember his own state of mind when he was the one ordering stones to be thrown at believers? Paul was being falsely accused of the same crimes he had levied at others—and he was receiving the same punishment.

Paul's accusations against others took him to Damascus (Acts 9:3). En route, he met Jesus, which was an experience that forever changed his life. Maybe the words of Jesus in that encounter came back to him as he lay at death's door outside the city of Lystra. On the Damascus road Jesus said, *Get up and stand on your feet. I have . . . appoint[ed] you . . . as a witness* (Acts 26:16). It appears that Paul responded to that same voice as he lay outside the city limits. He got up, stood on his feet, and went back into the city to be a witness of God's power. Jesus brings spiritual as well as physical healing so that we might be witnesses to His goodness. It is time to stand on our feet and walk in the pathway of His grace.

6. Look up the following scriptures. What did Jesus do for the lame?

   a. Matthew 11:5

   b. Matthew 15:30-31

   c. Matthew 21:14

7. When Elizabeth gave birth to John the Baptist, her husband, Zechariah, was filled with the Holy Spirit and prophesied (Luke 1:67-79). At the end of the prophecy he stated that God's tender mercy would guide what? (See verse 79.)

8. We might be emotionally "lame" because we have been injured by the actions or words of others. We might be spiritually lame because we have participated in injuring another. Is there anything for which you need God's healing touch? If so, write it below, and ask for His healing so that you might walk in His path of peace.

MEMORY CHALLENGE

Include the Memory Challenge in one of your prayers today.

DAY FIVE

Determined Feet

Read Acts 14:21-25.

1. To what towns did Paul and Barnabas return?

2. *a.* What happened to Paul in Antioch? (See Acts 13:50.)

   b. What happened to Paul in Iconium? (See Acts 14:5.)

   c. What happened to Paul in Lystra? (See Acts 14:19.)

3. *a.* What happened regarding the Word of the Lord in Antioch? (See Acts 13:49, 52.)

   b. What happened regarding the Word of the Lord in Iconium? (See Acts 14:1.)

   c. What happened with the Good News in Derbe after Paul and Barnabas left Lystra? (See Acts 14:21.)

4. Returning to a place where people have insulted, mistreated, or persecuted you takes a great deal of courage. Paul seemed undaunted by what others might do to him. He had determined that his feet would take him wherever God led. He lived out the truth that John proclaimed in 1 John 4:4. Write that truth below.

Paul went back into the city of Lystra to show the people there that the God he was proclaiming was able not only to do miracles but also to keep His servants alive when others wanted them dead. Paul and Barnabas then left Lystra and went to the nearby city of Derbe. Nothing that happened in Lystra, or in the other cities they visited, was able to quiet their testimony. They continued to preach the gospel and won a large number of disciples there. Derbe was as far east as they would go on this trip. It was time to consider their return to Antioch in Syria. They decided to retrace their steps through the regions of Galatia, Phrygia, Pisidia, and Pamphylia. One would think they might be weary of opposition and consider another route to avoid further conflict. But they had confidence in God's love and power to protect them, and they knew there was more work to do before they could go home. They went back, not just because the cities were on the route but also because they loved the people to whom God had called them to minister. They knew they would encounter some who hated them, but others would rejoice: those who put their faith in Jesus. They were grateful that many heard their message and obeyed. New life in Christ was a reality, but nurturing that new life was just as important. The missionaries desired to care for them like responsible parents who nurture their children.

The Gentiles needed special attention. They did not have the spiritual advantages Paul and Barnabas had when they came to Christ. Both Paul and Barnabas were devout Jews who received godly training in their youth, and both were familiar with the Scriptures. These advantages provided protection for them against the deceitful ways of Satan. Paul and Barnabas would not abandon these new babes in Christ, so they went back to Lystra, Iconium, and Antioch to teach them more about the Scriptures and to identify teachers and leaders who could carry on this ministry.

Their return was not just for the sake of convenience. If that were the case, they would have passed through (perhaps by night) but never would have gone again. We will discover, as we study further in Acts, that Paul went back again and again.

5. What two things did Paul and Barnabas do for the disciples (believers) in the cities to which they returned? (See 14:22.)

6. Paul described in 2 Timothy 4:17 what the Lord did for him. How might Paul's experience be similar to yours?

7. Read Romans 12:14-21. Paul wrote these admonitions sometime after his experiences in Acts 14. How do you think Paul's enemies might have responded to him as he attempted to live out these words?

8. What relationship might there be between the action prescribed in Romans 12 and your answers to question 3 above?

MEMORY CHALLENGE

With whom were we sealed for the day of redemption?

DAY SIX

Beautiful Feet

Read Acts 14:26-28.

1. Paul and Barnabas had been on a trip that took them through many towns and cities. The end of this journey is described in Acts 14:26. Where does the journey end?

2. The description of the start of this journey is found at the beginning of Acts 13. Where did the journey begin, and how were Paul and Barnabas sent off?

3. What had Paul and Barnabas reported to the believers that God had done in the places they had visited? (See Acts 14:27.)

The preaching of Paul and Barnabas challenged the new converts. New believers were told the truth, not vain promises of health, wealth, and ease. They would need enduring strength in the days ahead, so Paul and Barnabas appointed elders for each church to oversee the care of these new converts. After praying and fasting, they committed the converts to the nurture of the elders and to the care of the Lord.

Paul and Barnabas then returned to Antioch and stayed a long time with the other disciples. They reported the many good things that God had done. They likely spoke of some of the persecution that took place, or the stoning that nearly ended Paul's life. However, we have no record that they complained of any of that. Instead, we find that they gathered the church together to tell about how the Gentiles were coming to faith in Christ. The Gentiles had heard the Good News, had received that Good News, and now Paul and Barnabas were reporting good news back to the other disciples. The hope provided in the message of salvation and the forgiveness of sins is transformational. It is a powerful force that changes people's lives everywhere it is received.

Several years ago a friend of mine was visiting a town with which he had little familiarity. He was raised in a church-going family but had found that the teachings of the church were too restrictive for the life he wanted to lead. However, he felt impressed to visit a church in the town he was visiting. He decided to walk to a small church that he knew was holding an evening service. He put on his old tennis shoes and set out on the journey. When he arrived, the service had just begun. Apparently this evening was set aside for a men's Bible study, for only a group of men were gathered at the church. They invited him to come in and join them. He listened to familiar phases and familiar scriptures, but nothing was particularly moving to him.

After some time had passed, the leader of the group began to introduce a ritual that my friend knew was going to make him incredibly uncomfortable. The gathering was going to close in a foot-washing. An elderly gentleman came over and knelt before my friend and asked permission to wash his feet. Steve was very reluctant, but the elderly man was gently persistent and convincing. Steve was mortified, because he was wearing his old, smelly tennis shoes and could only imagine what his athletic socks and feet smelled like after the long walk. The man did not seem to notice but instead offered to Steve, through the foot-washing, an overture of love and acceptance. Steve told me that tears filled his eyes and he became overwhelmed with the truth of God's grace, forgiveness, and love. The gesture of the elderly gentleman was a gesture of good news. And through it Steve's smelly calloused feet were transformed into a symbol of God's grace.

4. Look up Isaiah 52:7. Write it in your own words below.

5. Read Romans 10:14-15. What is impossible for the person who has not heard the Good News?

6. Go to Romans 1:1 and determine who wrote the Book of Romans.

7. How do you think Romans 10:14-15 describes Paul's own experience? Relate your answer to what you have studied in Acts 14.

8. Listed below are the six lesson titles for this week. Pick one that best describes you, and explain why you have chosen that one.

   Dusty Feet

   Crippled Feet

   Mistaken Feet

   Healed Feet

   Determined Feet

   Beautiful Feet

9. List two ways in which you could be "beautiful feet" for someone else in the coming week.

MEMORY CHALLENGE

Use the memory verse in a prayer for yourself and for others.

Acts

■ A Study of Acts 15

LESSON 13

DAY ONE

Fallen from Grace

Read Acts 15, focusing on verses 1-4.

1. What were the men from Judea teaching? (See verse 1.)

2. What was the response of Paul and Barnabas? (See verse 2.)

Paul and Barnabas had experienced great success in sharing the good news of salvation by faith in Jesus Christ. In spite of the persecution the two of them experienced, the Gentiles were hearing the message, and a large number were being won to the Lord. As Acts 15 begins, Paul and Barnabas are back in Antioch. Here they were confronted with a major controversy that threatened to divide the young church and undermine the work that Paul and Barnabas had just completed.

Jews from Judea had come to Antioch and were teaching that circumcision, in the manner that Moses taught, was a necessary prerequisite to salvation. Paul was so adamantly opposed to this teaching that the believers in Antioch sent Paul, and some others, to Jerusalem to address the issue with the apostles and elders.

Paul's strong stance against the requirement of circumcision is recorded in the fifth chapter of his letter to the Galatians. There he states that anyone who re-creates the law in an attempt to be justified by that law has separated himself or herself from Christ. To re-create the law is to fall away from grace (Galatians 5:4). This is the only time that the writers of the Bible use the phrase "fallen from grace." However, it is a very important reference, because the distinction establishes that salvation is the free gift of God to all who believe, not given because of what they achieve.

Paul knew that the teaching he was hearing about circumcision was false. It was not compatible with the gospel he received by revelation from God, and he would not be disobedient to that revelation even if it meant standing alone.

The false teaching of circumcision as a necessary prerequisite to salvation had spread to Antioch. The doctrine had the potential to undermine church fellowship. Jews might avoid associating with uncircumcised Gentiles. Men who had been eating and worshiping together without incident might now be divided and confused. Apparently the church leaders were also divided on this issue, but they were united in wanting to know if the teaching was true or false. Before His death, Jesus had prayed for the unity of His followers (John 17). He knew they would face problems like this. Every generation faces problems.

3. Read Genesis 17:9-14.
   a. What was to be the sign of the covenant between Abraham and God?

   b. Who was to be circumcised?

MEMORY CHALLENGE

Ephesians 4:31

Get rid of all bitterness, rage and anger, brawling and slander, along with every form of malice.

c. What would happen if a male was not circumcised?

d. How long was the covenant to last?

4. How does God describe the children of Israel to Moses in Exodus 32:7-9?

5. Read Deuteronomy 10:14-17. What does Moses say must be done to correct the problem of being stiff-necked?

6. *a.* According to Romans 2:28-29, what does Paul declare to be the circumcision that characterized a true Jew?

   b. From whom will a man with a circumcised heart receive praise?

7. Read Galatians 6:12. Paul gives two reasons as to why some Jews were trying to convince the Galatian Gentiles to be circumcised. What are they?

8. Are there any issues today that would be similar to the issue of circumcision in the first century? In other words, are there any behavioral expectations that we might inappropriately require of new believers?

9. Read Galatians 5:6. What is Paul's conclusion to the matter?

DAY TWO

The Law or Grace?

Read Acts 15:5-9.

1. Who was saying that the Gentiles needed to be circumcised? (See verse 5.)

2. In addition to being circumcised, what did they say the Gentiles should be required to do? (See verse 5.)

Those who belonged to the party of the Pharisees were influential and vocal. Their belief in Jesus as the Christ did not erase their experience as Pharisees. They were experts in the law. They held themselves and others to behavioral standards that included not only the laws of Leviticus but also laws and rules that they felt were implied by the Levitical law. The Pharisees were legalists, and it is difficult to escape legalistic roots. Accepting the gift of salvation and its corresponding freedom is difficult for anyone who has spent a lifetime trying to earn God's approval. The Pharisees could not let go of the false security they had in their own laws, and they were determined to impose those same expectations on others.

The leaders of the Church gathered in Jerusalem to discuss the controversy. When the meeting started, believers opposing Paul were quick to state their case: *The Gentiles must be circumcised and required to obey the Law of Moses* (verse 5). Immediately the room buzzed with pros and cons on this issue. Finally Peter stood to his feet, and the gathering quieted. Among believers, respect for this man was without question. They could not forget his words on the Day of Pentecost, the miracles God had performed through him, and his escape from prison. God had clearly established him as a leader and a valid spokesman regarding spiritual matters.

Earlier, when Peter told the Christian Jews about what had taken place at Cornelius's house, they rejoiced. However, time had passed, and problems had developed. The Jews had struggled to accept the Gentiles as equals before God. Many had gone back to their old habits and ways of thinking. Faith in Jesus Christ had given them joy and freedom from guilt, but the social changes that resulted were causing problems with their non-Christian friends and family members. Peter understood their fears and prejudices. When God showed him the vision on the housetop, it took Peter three times before he was able to accept this truth.

Peter reminded the group that he had been God's vessel in giving the message of the gospel to the Gentiles, who were not only acceptable to God but also chosen by Him. When God baptized the Gentiles with His Spirit, He did for them what the law of circumcision could never do: He purified their hearts by faith.

3. Read Romans 3:20.
   a. Who will be declared righteous by observing the law?

   b. What does the law do for us?

4. Read Romans 6:23.
   a. What is the consequence of any sin?

   b. How do we avoid eternal death?

5. In today's passage (Acts 15:5-9) we learn that when we receive the message of the gospel, God will give us the Holy Spirit. As a result of this gift, what happens to our hearts? (See verse 9.)

6. Put into your own words what the following scriptures say about a person with a pure heart.

   Psalm 24:3-5

   Proverbs 22:11

   Matthew 5:8

7. In 1 Timothy 1:3-5, what does Paul tell Timothy is the goal of his command, and how is this achieved?

8. Do you tend to pray more for changes in behavior than for a pure heart? How are the two related?

MEMORY CHALLENGE

According to the memory verse, list the six things of which you are to rid yourself.

DAY THREE

More Work or More Grace?

Read Acts 15:6-11, focusing on verses 10-11.

1. How are people saved?

2. What is the "yoke" that neither those in the meeting nor their fathers could bear?

I have a work associate who moved to our town from Kansas City. She leased an apartment in an area on the northwest side of town. Several of her friends drove with her from Kansas City to help her move all her belongings into her new place. They had to be close friends, because the apartment she rented was on the third floor—and there were no elevators!

I have moved several times and have discovered that there are very few items that one person and a good hand truck cannot handle. However, a Hide-a-Bed couch is another story. Navigating stairs and corners with a Hide-a-Bed can be a nightmare. If you have ever had one unfold while trying to twist it through a narrow hall or around a corner, then you know how funny and dangerous this task can be. My coworker from Kansas City had moved hers five times in three different cities. I believe she will admit that each time fewer and fewer friends volunteered to help.

Peter uses similar imagery in describing what some of the Jewish believers were expecting of the Gentile believers. He says they were forcing others to carry a yoke. Literally, a yoke is a heavy wooden bar harnessed to oxen to enable them to pull a plow. If his audience had been more familiar with moving furniture than moving plows, then he might have changed his word picture. He might have said that the Pharisees boasted of having a Hide-a-Bed couch in their homes but that the burden of trying to move it was greater than anyone could bear. And here they were requiring everyone to have a Hide-a-Bed couch. Having a heavy couch simply points toward the need for help, not toward the need for more couches. In the same way, the law points toward the need for grace, not toward the need for more laws. For it is through grace that our hearts are made pure. God works from the inside on the motivations of the heart. As He creates a pure heart, obedience will naturally follow.

3. In Matthew 23:27-28, what did Jesus call the Pharisees and teachers of the Law? Why?

4. How did Jesus describe the Pharisees and the teachers of the law in the following verses?
   a. Matthew 23:4

   b. Matthew 23:5

   c. Matthew 23:15

   d. Matthew 23:23

   e. Matthew 23:25

   f. Matthew 23:28

5. Before we are too judgmental of the Pharisees, we should ask if any of these descriptions are applicable to our own lives. Do any of the six descriptions above apply to you? If so, record them below.

6. The Holy Spirit lives within and changes our motives from within. He helped Peter change his hypocritical behavior. Peter's training had stressed the mandate to bring actions into harmony with the law. But now a higher law was in effect. Now motives of the heart had to be in harmony with God's law of love. God through the Holy Spirit accomplished that, and the Holy Spirit had written a new law on Peter's heart. He will do the same for us. Long ago, the psalmist prayed for this inward and outward harmony. Look up Psalm 19:14 and record it below. Allow God to bring your life into harmony with His love.

7. Use Psalm 51:10 as the basis for a prayer of your own.

MEMORY CHALLENGE

List a personal and specific example of at least four of the six things of which you are to rid yourself.

DAY FOUR

Graceful Leadership

Read Acts 15:5-21.

1. Who were gathered in the assembly to participate in the discussion?

2. What was the issue being debated? (See verse 5.)

3. Who are identified by name as individuals who spoke up on the issue? (See verses 7, 12-13.)

Peter concluded his words with a powerful statement of faith: *We believe it is through the grace of our Lord Jesus that we are saved, just as they are* (verse 11). Statements made by Barnabas and Paul followed this. They did not defend their position on Gentile circumcision but instead shared with their Christian brothers the wonderful things the Lord had done through their ministry among the Gentiles. Those who were truly interested in God's work, regardless of their views on the issue being debated, had to be thrilled to hear the details of His wonderful blessing among the Gentiles. Issues are usually seen from a more objective perspective when they are placed in the larger context of God's unfolding work. It is hard to recite your difficulties and praise the Lord at the same time.

James was the next to speak up. He was a pastor in Jerusalem, but more important for this issue, he was the presiding elder of the group that had gathered. He has since been called the bishop of Jerusalem and in this setting was responsible for pronouncing the definitive response on the debate. His task was difficult. The issue had resulted in strong differences in opinion. These differences could easily have divided the Church and turned the good news of the gospel into the bad news of bureaucracy. What was needed was strong, grace-filled leadership.

James rose to the occasion. He showed he was sensitive to the concerns of all parties by offering a solution that was acceptable to both Jews and Gentiles. He honored the historical context of their faith by pointing out that Peter's experience at Cornelius's house was consistent with the words of Amos the prophet, who foresaw God's acceptance of the Gentiles. He motivated the people by telling them they were witnessing God rebuilding *David's fallen tent* (verse 16). He showed compassion in insisting that the church *not make it difficult for the Gentiles who are turning to God* (verse 19). Agreement was reached, and the rules for the Gentiles were both reasonable and helpful.

Leadership is tested in conflict. James addressed this particular conflict with sensitivity, respect, inspiration, and compassion. He allowed the grace he had received through faith in Christ to saturate his role as leader of the church. Grace does not make one weak but instead empowers a person to lead with both conviction and compassion.

4. The council listened to the wisdom of God as revealed through James. Read what James said about wisdom in James 1:5-8, and answer the following questions:

   What should the person who lacks wisdom do?

   What will be God's response to that person?

   Will God blame the person for his or her lack of wisdom?

   What else is important?

5. What four things did James and the council ask the Gentile converts not to do? (See Acts 14:20.)

6. Of the four things listed above, one had to be addressed by Paul in his letter to the church at Corinth. Look up 1 Corinthians 8, and determine the issue.

Paul's admonition in 1 Corinthians 8:9 is a powerful guideline for believers. Write it below in your own words.

7. The conclusion of the matter was a compromise for the Gentiles as well as the Jews.

   According to Galatians 5:3, what did Paul indicate an adult Gentile convert was obligated to do if he allowed himself to be circumcised to appease the requirements of the Hebrew law?

   Read Matthew 5:17-18. What did Jesus say concerning the Law of Moses?

   Was the final decision a violation of either the Law of Moses or the law of grace? Why or why not?

8. Is there a division in your church that has bothered you? What could you do to promote graceful leadership regarding the issue?

MEMORY CHALLENGE

Recite the Memory Challenge to a friend.

DAY FIVE

The Blessing Grace

Read Acts 15:22-35.

1. Who did the council send to Antioch?

2. What did the council send to the Gentile believers?

3. When the delegations arrived in Antioch, what was the first thing they did?

4. Who besides the apostles and elders agreed the Gentiles should not be burdened with more than the rules contained in the letter?

5. How did the people in the Antioch church respond when the letter was read?

6. What did the brothers in Antioch do when it was time for their guests to return to Jerusalem?

7. Where did Paul and Barnabas go, and what did they do when Judas and Silas returned to Jerusalem?

8. Were they the only ones doing this?

Good communication is not always easy. On the university campus where I worked until recently, chapel services are conducted from 10:50 A.M. to 11:30 A.M. On more than one occasion I would tell guest speakers that our services begin at "ten till eleven." Some interpreted that to mean that chapel begins at 10 A.M. and goes until 11 A.M. Though this simple misunderstanding has minor consequences, similar miscommunications have had horrendous consequences. In 1974 a plane crash killing 92 passengers occurred when the pilot misunderstood the air traffic controller's expression "You are cleared for approach."[1] Written communication can be as confusing as verbal communication. An exit sign on one Oklahoma City's expressways indicates that Route 3 East and 44 West are the same road. If the traveler on that road is not sufficiently confused by the claim that he or she is simultaneously traveling in opposite directions, the problem will worsen with one glance at the compass, which will indicate that the vehicle is traveling neither east nor west—but south!

The Antioch church had asked for help from the apostles in Jerusalem. Now the apostles had to convey their decision in such a way that the Gentiles there would receive it as it was intended and realize their answer was prompted by love. They decided to send both a letter and some of their own leaders from the church in Jerusalem with the delegation from Antioch. They wanted to make sure the believers heard their message and their motive.

The apostles and elders in the Jerusalem church composed the letter. It began with a word of greeting that literally means, "We wish you to be well" or "We desire you to be safe."[2] These people had been waiting quite a while to hear the decision regarding their circumcision controversy. The opening salutation set the stage by indicating the desire of the church leaders to foster unity, not division; safety, not uncertainty; healing, not hostility.

The content of the letter discredited the false teachers. Paul and Barnabas were affirmed as dear friends and faithful teachers. Judas and Silas were introduced to confirm the message of the letter. The salutation expressed the intent that the decision be a blessing, a blessing that would enable the believers to rejoice. The desire of the church leaders was fulfilled. The Gentiles were glad and encouraged. When Judas and Silas left, they were given a blessing of peace. The church leaders, led by the Holy Spirit, offered grace in the same way it had been given to them and produced a blessing of great joy.

MEMORY CHALLENGE

Set your alarm clock to the time that corresponds to the Scripture reference. When the alarm goes off, recite the Memory Challenge.

DAY SIX

In Spite of Grace

Read Acts 15:36-41.

1. Where did Paul want to go, and what did he want to do? (See verse 36.)

2. Who did Barnabas want to bring along? (See verse 37.)

3. Acts 13:13 describes the previous experience Paul and Barnabas had with John Mark. Describe what happened.

This chapter tells of the way a conflict between the Jews and the Gentiles was solved by an acceptable compromise. Incredibly, in the same chapter Dr. Luke tells us about a personal controversy between friends and Christian brothers that ended in division.

Paul wanted to go back to visit the Christian brothers in all the places where he and Barnabas had preached the Word of the Lord. Paul's wealth of knowledge in the Scriptures and Barnabas with his gift of compassion would strengthen the new converts in their faith.

They both wanted to go, but neither would agree on whom to take with them. Paul did not want to take John Mark along, and Barnabas would not go without him. No doubt Paul wanted proof that Mark was committed to the work. Last time, he quit before the work in Asia began. However, Barnabas insisted that John Mark be part of the travel team. Neither man really understood the other's position on the issue of John Mark.

Paul was a strong, forceful leader and was likely unaccustomed to Barnabas's strength of resolution. No doubt he was aware that Barnabas felt he was being unduly harsh in his judgment of John Mark, especially in light of the fact that Paul's past behavior had not been exactly exemplary. Barnabas probably expected Paul to be more merciful.

We do not know if Barnabas advised Paul or the church that he and John Mark were leaving Antioch and going to Cyprus. We simply know that Barnabas was heading home. The story line, which introduced him back in chapter 4 as a Levite from Cyprus, ends in chapter 16 as Paul and Barnabas separate. They were in such sharp disagreement that compromise was apparently impossible. It must have been an emotional time for both of them.

The author of Acts, Dr. Luke, becomes part of the story in the next chapter. He must have learned about this breech in relationship as he traveled with Paul. This was a difficult issue, a painful conflict, an unresolved disagreement. Maybe the Holy Spirit preserved the account so that we would not romanticize the Early Church or have an idealistic notion of how God works. However, the story does not end with this chapter. Often God uses time as an instrument of His grace.

4. What does Paul say was a basis for his decision to not take John Mark?

5. Can you see any good that God was able to bring out of this irreconcilable difference of opinion? In what ways do you think Paul was justified in his position? What defense can you give for Barnabas?

6. What should our attitude be when we have a difference of opinion with a Christian brother? Read Colossians 3:12-17 for help in answering.

7. Read 2 Timothy 4:11. What compliment did Paul give John Mark?

8. Have you ever differed with someone else's opinions or choices? If so, record who it was and why you disagreed with him or her.

9. *a.* Is there a person with whom you have had an unresolved disagreement and with whom there is now very little communication?

   b. Has your need to be "right" been more important than your desire to remain in "relationship"?

   c. Pray for yourself and for the other person.

MEMORY CHALLENGE

Try to recite the Memory Challenge along with the two previous memory verses (Ephesians 4:29-31).

Wisdom of the Word **Bible Study Series**

Acts

■ A Study of Acts 16—17

LESSON 14

DAY ONE

Stopped by the Spirit

Read Acts 16, focusing on verses 1-12.

The previous chapter ends with Paul embarking on his second missionary journey. He specifically did not take along a young man by the name of John Mark. Chapter 16 begins in one of the first towns in which Paul and his companions stopped. In the city of Lystra Paul met another young man, a disciple by the name of Timothy.

1. List all the information we are given about Timothy (Acts 16:1-3).

2. Why did Paul have Timothy circumcised?

3. How do you explain Paul's actions given his stance in Acts 15:1-2?

4. Timothy's mother was a follower of Jesus and a Jew, but his father was Greek. Paul wanted Timothy to join his group on their journey, and apparently Timothy wanted to go. Paul decided to have him circumcised. He considered being uncircumcised a handicap for their work, because much of the work would be among unbelieving Jews. Jews would consider Timothy unclean and would also consider Paul unclean for associating with him. Timothy was willing. Paul would not have done this if both Timothy's parents were Gentile. Such was the case with Titus. Look up Galatians 2:3-5, and write Paul's response to that situation.

As they traveled westward Paul saw people everywhere with whom he wanted to share the gospel, but the Holy Spirit restrained him. God was teaching His servants to wait for direction. Paul saw opportunity everywhere, but when he tried to enter certain places, the Holy Spirit opposed him. The issue was not Paul's willingness but rather his need for direction. Paul obeyed the Spirit. One might wonder if he ever became anxious or distracted by the expectations of his comrades. At any rate, they continued until they finally came to Troas, on the shore of the Great Sea. With closed doors behind them and no direction as to what their next move should be, they waited.

For people who like to reflect and think things through, action can be frightening. For those who like to take action, waiting can be frustrating. I had a Sunday School teacher who once described the Holy Spirit as being like the rudder of a ship. The rudder turns the boat to

MEMORY CHALLENGE

Ephesians 4:32

Be kind and compassionate to one another, forgiving each other, just as in Christ God forgave you.

the left or the right, but it does not do anything if the ship is not moving. Sometimes we need to move ahead by faith and trust that God will lead us. On the other hand, there are people who never stop to consider the consequences of certain actions and as a result often leave a trail of brokenness in the path they walk. Just because an opportunity exists does not mean that it is a good choice. God has something to teach both those who naturally act and those who naturally wait. Waiting on God for direction is equally as important as seeking His blessing and guidance on action that has already been taken.

Paul was confident of this one thing: the Christ who called him to preach to the Gentiles would show him where he should go, and He did.

During the night Paul had a vision giving him specific direction. He was to cross the sea into Europe. A man in Macedonia was calling for help. Just as God prepared Peter through a vision to go to the house of Cornelius and prepared Ananias to go to Saul, the Lord now showed Paul a man in Macedonia ready to receive the gospel. The Lord promises to go before us as we serve Him. He prepares the way. He makes hearts ready to receive the truth, and He looks for servants like Paul who wait for direction and then take action.

5. What was the primary purpose of this second trip? (See Acts 16:4.)

   What was the response to the decision reached by the apostles and elders in Jerusalem? (See verse 5.)

6. Into what areas was Paul not permitted to go?

   What area did he pass by?

   Who would not allow Paul to preach in Asia or enter Bithynia?

7. Do you find it harder to wait or to take action?

   What might God teach you if you tried to do more of what you answered in part *a*?

8. Write a scripture that speaks about waiting on God.

   Write a scripture that speaks about taking action.

9. This chapter began with an introduction to the disciple Timothy from the town of Lystra. The group eventually made their way to a Roman colony in the district of Macedonia. What city is it? (See verse 12.)

10. Paul would one day write a letter to the church in this town. In it he talks about Timothy. Look up Philippians 2:19-22. What does Paul say about Timothy?

DAY TWO

A Discerning Spirit

Read Acts 16:10-18.

1. The pronouns used in verse 10 are significantly different that those used in all the previous chapters. What two pronouns are used that have not been used before?

2. What does this change imply?

Up to this point, the author of the Book of Acts has written from the perspective of a historian or reporter who has gathered facts and information from eyewitnesses or from other authors and put together an account of what others had seen and experienced. Beginning with Acts 16:10, it appears that the author, Dr. Luke, joins the group and becomes an eyewitness himself of the events about which he writes. Much like the current practice of reporters being embedded with the military troops stationed overseas and actually observing the battles as they take place, so Luke is embedded with Paul's evangelistic team and observes the spiritual warfare firsthand.

When Paul and the group discerned where God was leading, they left immediately for Macedonia and went to a leading city in that district called Philippi. Not many Jews settled there because it was a Roman colony. It was customary for a synagogue to be established where 10 Jewish men were in residence, but none existed in Philippi. So on the Sabbath, the missionary team went out to the riverside, where they expected to find a place for prayer. Some women had gathered by the river. When they began talking with these women, they discovered that one was a true worshiper of God. She was a successful businesswoman whose name was Lydia. Afterward she and her household were baptized. And she graciously asked the missionaries to stay in her home while they remained in Philippi.

3. On a subsequent occasion, again on their way to prayer, they met a slave girl who was possessed of a spirit whereby she was able to tell fortunes. She followed the group and shouted statements that were true. What was she shouting?

4. True statements are not always said with right motives. Read Mark 1:21-27 and answer the following questions.
   a. Where was Jesus, and what was He doing?

   b. What was the response of the people to His teaching?

   c. Who cried out, and what did he say?

   d. Was what the man said incorrect?

   e. What were Jesus' two commands?

The slave girl continued her practice for days. Paul discerned that what she was doing was not right and confronted the spirit that was within her.

5. Many people consider some of the practices listed in Deuteronomy 18:9-12 as innocent recreation. What does scripture say about them?

6. Read Isaiah 8:19. From whom are we to seek guidance?

7. In whose name did Paul command the spirit to come out of the slave girl?

God does not provide discernment just for the purpose of confronting something troubling in others. He also provides discernment so that we might check our own motives. We must remember that just because something *can* be said does not mean it *should* be said.

Just because something is true does not necessarily make it right to say. And just because the words are correct does not guarantee that the motives are pure. We must learn when to speak and when to remain silent. A wise man once offered this standard: "Is what I am about to say an improvement over the silence?"

8. Look up the following scriptures and write what they mean to you:

   1 Kings 3:9

   Job 33:31-33

   Proverbs 17:28

   Ecclesiastes 3:1, 7

   Zechariah 8:16-17

   Acts 18:9

MEMORY CHALLENGE

What are three characteristics we should have toward others?

DAY THREE

Freedom in the Spirit

Read Acts 16:19-34.

1. Today's passage of Scripture depicts a powerful contrast between being enslaved and being free. Listed below are several characters mentioned in this passage. Based on the story, write a way in which each is in bondage and a way in which each is free.

   The slave girl

   The slave girl's owners

   Paul and Silas

   Other prisoners

   The jailer and his family

The continuous shouting of the slave girl troubled Paul. Eventually he commanded the spirit to come out of her. The spirit obeyed. She might still be a slave to her owners, but her heart was set free by Paul's command. Now, however, her owners were furious. Paul had destroyed the only value they found in the girl. They seized Paul and Silas and took them to the authorities. They were charged with causing a civil disturbance. The magistrates had them stripped and beaten and thrown into prison.

The sudden turn of events probably did not surprise Paul, but Silas might have been stunned by how quickly they landed in jail, bloody, bruised, and beaten. They were just going to the riverside to pray, and now they were shackled in a dark cell. Paul may have reminded Silas that since their prayer time had been interrupted, they now had time to resume their prayers. Their bodies may have been in bondage, but their spirits were free to pray. As they did, perhaps Jesus reminded them that He knew just how it felt to be beaten by Roman soldiers. Or maybe He reminded them of what He said to His followers: *Blessed are those who are persecuted because of righteousness, for theirs is the kingdom of heaven* (Matthew 5:10). Anyway, during prayer, pain gave way to praise as they began to sing. Maybe it was one of David's songs or a hymn of the Early Church, but whatever it was, it caught the attention of the other prisoners. Many sounds had filled the old prison as darkness descended each night, but they probably had never heard singing like this. As if the earth were applauding the prison concert, a violent earthquake shook the structure to its foundation. The doors flew open, and the prisoners' chains fell off. Spiritual freedom had produced physical freedom.

What followed next is a remarkable look at God preparing a man to receive the gospel message. When the jailer, who was awakened by the violent quake, saw the prison doors opened, he panicked, jumping to a wrong conclusion. He was certain the prisoners were gone. Miraculously, no one had left, but the jailer did not know it. He was certain he would be held responsible for the escape of the prisoners. He would be thrown into prison, subjected to public disgrace, and possibly executed. Suicide seemed a preferable alternative.

Somehow Paul knew what the jailer was going to do and shouted for him to stop. The jailer, trembling from the events, fell before Paul and Silas and asked for the same freedom these prisoners had. What an irony! Before the night was over, the jailer and all his family were baptized. The experience of Paul and Silas shows that anyplace can become a sanctuary of worship when we surrender our spirits to the freedom God offers in Christ Jesus.

2. Who ordered Paul and Silas beaten?

3. List all that Paul and Silas suffered in verses 22-24.

4. There are many ways in which we can feel physically bound or enslaved. Can you name some ways you have experienced?

5. Write Paul's answer to the jailer's question "What must I do to be saved?"

6. What is our responsibility in helping others experience more freedom?

7. There are many ways in which we can feel emotionally, intellectually, or spiritually bound or enslaved. Can you name some of the ways in which you might have experienced this type of bondage? How has God's grace helped you in some of these areas?

8. Is there an area in which you still feel in bondage? Could you make it a matter of prayer this week?

MEMORY CHALLENGE

Personalize the memory verse. List the names of some individuals to whom you need to exhibit the traits listed in the memory verse.

DAY FOUR

Joy in the Spirit

Read Acts 16:33-40.

1. What was the magistrate's original order? (See Acts 16:22.)

2. What was the magistrate's new order? (See verse 35.)

3. What did Paul want? (See verse 37.)

Paul and Silas had been mistreated, but more significantly, the message they proclaimed had been maligned. The two of them had been accused of criminal activity, and the new believers would be affected by their association with Paul and Silas. Paul did not want to simply get out of jail—he wanted their reputation cleared. He did not want revenge. If that were his motive, as a Roman citizen he could appeal to a higher authority to correct the injustice. Instead, it appears he simply wanted to be cleared of all of the charges and for the local authorities to respect the legitimacy of this new group of believers.

4. List all of the possible converts in Philippi who are mentioned in chapter 16.

   Verses 14-15

   Possibly verse 18

   Possibly verse 25

   Verses 33-34

   Possibly verse 40

5. With what were the jailer and his family filled? (See verse 34.)

Approximately nine years after these events took place, Paul would write a letter to the believers at Philippi. Likely the recipients of the letter included the jailer and his household, and Lydia and her household. It appears that Paul's experience with the jailer's family became a hallmark of the Church. Their experience of joy became a theme that is woven throughout the letter to the Philippians.[1]

6. Look up Philippians 1:4. When Paul prayed for the believers at Philippi, how did he pray?

The letter to the Philippians was likely written during Paul's imprisonment in Rome. Who would better understand how God could work through Paul's imprisonment and chains of bondage than the jailer and the other believers in Philippi? They saw firsthand how God used a prison stay to advance His divine purposes. Paul had friends in Philippi who would be empathetic and would lift him up in prayer.

7. What is similar between Philippians 1:12-13 and Acts 16:25 and 33?

8. What effect did Paul's prison behavior have on other believers? (See Philippians 1:14 and Acts 16:40.)

9. What effect do you think your behavior, when you are faced with difficult circumstances, has on other people?

10. Paul has confidence in ______ _______ of the believers in Philippi (Philippians 1:19).

MEMORY CHALLENGE

Say the Memory Challenge aloud six times: three by reading and three by memory.

DAY FIVE

Protected by the Spirit

Read Acts 17, focusing on verses 1-15.

1. What did Paul and Silas find in Thessalonica?

2. What was Paul's customary practice?

The missionaries left Philippi and traveled 70 to 100 miles west to Thessalonica. They would take the better part of a week to walk that distance. It is doubtful that Luke was with them, since details of the trip are missing and the pronouns "we" and "us" are not found in this portion of the text.

Thessalonica was a thriving commercial center and capital of Macedonia located on the Aegean Sea. At the synagogue, Paul was graciously received as a trained rabbi. He reasoned from the Scriptures, on three consecutive Sabbaths, proving that Jesus was the Messiah. We do not know what his arguments were, but they might have been similar to his arguments found in Romans 4—6. He proved from the Scriptures that what the prophets had foretold would happen. As Paul reasoned, the Holy Spirit did His work of convincing. As a result, some Jews, many God-fearing Greeks, and some prominent women believed.

The jealous unbelieving Jews incited a mob, and a riot broke out. They stormed the house where the missionaries were staying. However, they failed to find Paul and Silas. We do not know where Paul and Silas were. All we know is that the mob did not find them. They were protected from the riot.

There are certainly many times that God watches over us, and we may be unaware of His protection. I have a ritual with my youngest daughter. When she crawls into bed at night, I pray for us, and then before I leave the room she asks, "No bad things?" I reply, "No. No bad things." I am grateful that so far in my young girl's life there have been no bad things to invade her nighttime slumber.

My older daughter is now 16. There is no end to the number of things that can concern the father of a teenage girl. A few weeks ago her best friend dropped her off at the house. Five minutes later, less than a mile from our home, that friend was in a terrible three-car accident. Fortunately no one was injured. However, the passenger side where my daughter had been riding five minutes earlier was severely crushed.

I do not know why tragic accidents happen to some people and not to others. I do not know why terrible illnesses fall on some and not on others. I do not know why Paul and Silas were thrown in prison in Philippi but spared from that fate in Thessalonica, nor why Jason went to prison in their stead. I just believe it is good to regularly thank God for His protective care—protecting us more than we could ever realize.

3. Where did the brothers in Thessalonica send Paul and Silas? (See Acts 17:10.)

4. How did the Bereans measure Paul's truthfulness? (See verse 11.)

5. What did the Thessalonica Jews do in Berea? (See verse 13.)

6. Where did the brothers send Paul? (See verse 14.)

7. Can you list a time you felt God protected you or a family member?

8. Write a prayer of thanksgiving for the many times for which there have been "no bad things."

MEMORY CHALLENGE

Include the Memory Challenge as part of saying grace before today's meals.

DAY SIX

The Spirit and Wisdom

Read Acts 17:16-34.

1. What distressed Paul about Athens? (See Acts 17:16.) As a Jew, why would it bother him so much?

2. Where did Paul engage in dialogue? (See verse 17.)

3. How did the residents of Athens spend their time? (See verse 21.)

Discussing the latest ideas is very intoxicating—but not necessarily productive. Yet this was at the heart of the Athenian life. Athens was the cultural center of the world. Art, literature, oratory, and religion were the things that had made this city famous. It was the home of Socrates and Plato and the adopted home of Aristotle, Epicurus, and Zeno. It was also the cradle of democracy. Out of respect for her history and accomplishments, the Romans left Athens as a free city to pursue her own goals. It was famous for mathematics, philosophy, and architecture. The Greeks gave the world a love not only of knowledge and beauty but also of freedom. But with all the things that recommended this center of civilization, it was spiritually bankrupt. They knew nothing of salvation. Greek philosophy discovered many truths but could not find the Truth. Neither human knowledge nor intellectualism in and of itself is capable of finding God.

Paul saw it all as he walked the streets and realized again that humanity without Christ is hopelessly lost. The great city was involved in idolatry, and Paul knew Satan had succeeded in deceiving her into the worship of powerless idols, degrading behavior, and superstition. It broke his heart to see what happens when people believe a lie, but he did not despair. He was there by God's grace and providence to present the truth of Jesus Christ.

4. How did Paul compliment the Athenians? (See verse 22.)

5. What did Paul find as he walked around the city observing their objects of worship that he proposed to tell them about? (See verse 23.)

6. How can we worship God with our minds?

7. Read James 3:13-17. What kind of "wisdom" is unspiritual?

   What are the characteristics of wisdom that comes from heaven?

8. What was the response to Paul's words? (See Acts 17:32-34.)

Even against the odds of Athens, Paul knew that nothing is impossible with God. He went first to the synagogue and reasoned with the Jews and God-fearing Greeks and next to the marketplace. Finally, he was in the Areopagus before the powerful council there. They wanted to hear what he had to say. In a city that exalted knowledge and prized intellectual excellence, Paul described their notions of the divine as "ignorant" (verse 30). What an affront to a prideful group of people! But without shame he called the proud men of Athens to repentance.

MEMORY CHALLENGE

Ask a friend or family member to test you on reciting the Memory Challenge (and Ephesians 4:29-31).

Wisdom of the Word Bible Study Series

Acts

■ A Study of Acts 18-19

LESSON 15

DAY ONE

Love and Marriage

Read Acts 18, focusing on verses 1-5.

The Lord led Paul from Athens on to Corinth. At this time in history, Corinth was the chief commercial city of Greece. It was located about 50 miles west of Athens on a strip of land that joined northern and southern Greece. Because of its strategic location for both land transportation and shipping routes, it was a key city for trade between Asia and Rome. The ancient city of Corinth was destroyed by the Romans in 146 B.C. However, it was restored by Julius Caesar about 100 years later. Corinth was the seat of government for southern Greece; therefore, a Roman proconsul resided there (see Acts 18:12).

The temple of Aphrodite (or Venus) stood on the Corinthians Acropolis. It is said that a thousand prostitutes were housed in this temple and participated in the licentious worship of this sex goddess. Eventually this city's name would become synonymous with immorality or fornication.[1]

Timothy and Silas eventually joined Paul in Corinth. They had stayed behind in Berea and had apparently been helping the churches in that area. The report they gave regarding the churches was very encouraging to Paul.

The report from Timothy apparently inspired Paul to write his first letter to the Thessalonians while he was still in Corinth.

Right in the middle of all the moral pollution of Corinth, Paul found a Jewish synagogue in which to teach and two friends with whom to live and work. Aquila and his wife, Priscilla, were tentmakers who had come recently to Corinth because the Emperor Claudius had banished Jews from Rome. They welcomed Paul and offered him a place to stay and a place to work. Aquila and Priscilla are a wonderful example not only of how God works *in* a marriage but also of how He can work *through* a marriage. Some couples capitalize on each other's strengths, minimize each other's weaknesses, compliment each other in ministry, and find it easy to work side by side. Their united efforts seem to be more productive than if they were to work separately. Aquila and Priscilla were such a couple. They are never mentioned separately in the Bible. In marriage and ministry, they were together.

In an age when the focus is mostly on what happens *between* a husband and wife, Aquila and Priscilla are an example of what can happen *through* a husband and wife. Their effectiveness together speaks about their relationship with each other. Their hospitality opened the doorway of salvation to many. They are a reminder that the Christian home is still one of the best tools for spreading the gospel.

The city of Corinth, with its worship of the goddess Aphrodite, often caused people to separate physical intimacy from spiritual or emotional intimacy. In contrast, Priscilla and Aquila show how a godly marriage can be a means of grace both to the marriage partners and to the people with whom they come in contact. There is the possibility that the wonderful admonitions of sacrificial love and mutual submission that Paul gives to married partners might have been influenced by the love he saw in the relationship of Priscilla and Aquila.

1. The Book of Romans was likely written by Paul during his second visit to Corinth. He would have been surrounded by the immorality and perversions of that town as he wrote to the Romans. Read Romans 1:24-31.
   a. In verse 28, what did the people think was not worthwhile?

MEMORY CHALLENGE

Ephesians 5:1

Be imitators of God, therefore, as dearly loved children.

b. To what did God give them over?

c. Instead of their hearts being filled with the Holy Spirit, list the things that filled them (verse 29).

d. How does Paul describe their character in verses 30-31?

2. Look up the following scriptures and list some of the characteristics of Aquila and Priscilla.
   a. Acts 18:2
   b. Acts 18:26
   c. Romans 16:3
   d. 1 Corinthians 16:19

3. In Ephesians 5 Paul describes the Christian marriage.
   a. In verse 21, what does Paul say we do out of reverence for Christ?
   b. How are husbands to love their wives? (See verse 25.)
   c. How did Christ show His love for the Church?
   d. How is the radiant church described in verse 27?

4. Name a way by which the struggles and problems of a marriage can be used as an instrument of God in showing His love to others.

DAY TWO

Love and Fear

Read Acts 18:6-22.

1. When Paul left the synagogue, where did he go? (See verse 7.)

2. Who were some of the new converts? (See verse 8.)

3. Paul had come from Athens where he conversed with people who spent their time doing nothing but talking about and listening to the latest ideas (Acts 17:21). Apparently God used that experience in Paul's life to mold the way he would try to persuade the Corinthians. Read 1 Corinthians 2:1-2.
   a. How did Paul not present himself?
   b. What was the sole focus of Paul's message?

4. Paul was afraid. He may have been taken aback by the experience in the synagogue or afraid that what had happened to him in previous cities might happen again, or he may have simply been fearful of the responsibility of proclaiming the message of faith in Christ. How does Paul describe himself in regard to his visit to Corinth? (See 1 Corinthians 2:3.)

God prepares His children for what they must face. He wants them to live with confidence in His wisdom, His power, and His love. Down across the history of God's relationship with humanity, He has assisted His children in various ways. God provides direction in what to do and gives assurance that He will abide with us as we walk in obedience.

It is a wonderful partnership: the child promises to obey, and God the Father promises to guide and protect. The difficult part of this relationship is that the child may not see the promised protection or power and must believe the Father's promise even when circumstances appear as if the promised protection and power are not coming. It is a love relationship that works by faith. The child promises to obey and believe the Father's word, and the Father promises to do just exactly what He says He will do.

Paul had been walking in this kind of relationship with the Lord. He had obeyed God all the way to Corinth. This had not been an easy assignment. The opposition and abuse from his fellow Jews was escalating. What was said of Jesus could also be said of Paul: *He came unto his own, and his own received him not* (John 1:11, KJV). The Lord knew Paul's thoughts and inward struggles and came to help His servant through a vision in the night. He calmed Paul's fears, affirmed his obedience, and assured him of His presence. God speaks to His children in a variety of ways. The more we become aware of His voice and the more certain we are of His abiding presence, the more our fears of surrounding circumstances will begin to disappear.

5. Answer the following questions based on Acts 18:9-10.
   a. What did the Lord say regarding Paul's fears?

   b. What did the Lord say that Paul should do to be obedient?

   c. What did the Lord say about His abiding presence?

   d. What did the Lord say about His protection?

   e. What did the Lord say about Paul's possible feelings of being alone?

6. According to Job 33:14, how does God speak?

7. Listed below are some of the ways in which God speaks. List an example of each, either from your own life or from Scripture. For instance, the first one listed is God's speaking through circumstances. In the passage of Acts we read today, God clarified Paul's calling to take the good news of the gospel to the Gentiles by allowing the opposition of the Jews in the synagogue (circumstances) to lead him to the conclusion that he was to take the Good News to the Gentiles.

   God speaks through circumstances.

   God speaks through nature.

   God speaks through the wise counsel of others.

   God speaks through His Word.

   God speaks through the intelligence He has given us.

   God speaks through our spirit-led intuition.

   God speaks through time.

8. When we become more aware of God's love, what happens to fear? (See 1 John 4:18.)

MEMORY CHALLENGE

Who should we imitate?

What kind of children are we?

DAY THREE

Love and Friendship

Read Acts 18:18-28.

1. Name the places, in order, that Paul visited. (See verses 18-23.)

2. Where did Paul leave Priscilla and Aquila?

3. Where did Apollos meet Priscilla and Aquila?

4. Where did Apollos go following his time with Priscilla and Aquila?

5. A Jew from Alexandria came to Ephesus. His name was Apollos. List as many characteristics of Apollos as you can find, explicit or implicit, in Acts 18:24-26.

Apollos was eloquent, mighty in the Scriptures, and accurate in his teaching. Speaking in front of a crowd can be intimidating. Even more intimidating is the assignment of trying to say something coherent about God. I understand that an old Hebrew saying goes like this: "The only thing we can say about God is that we really can't say anything about God." As soon as we say something about God, we tend to place Him in a "box"—and God is bigger than any box or definition we might try to impose on Him.

At the close of many of my sermons, I offer up a prayer that if I have said anything accurate and helpful, God would help the people to remember; and that whatever I have said that is not useful or is inaccurate, God would help us to forget it. I admire Apollos in that he *taught about Jesus accurately.* What a tragedy it is when Jesus is misrepresented, and what a blessing it is when He is accurately reflected in the teaching and life of His followers!

Another admirable quality of Apollos is described in verse 27. The text says that when Apollos went to Achaia, *he was a great help* to the believers. We have a family friend who invites us to stay in her home every time we are in her town. She never appears bothered by the hour of our arrival, the length of our stay, or the demands of our agenda. She always has a roast cooking in the oven, fresh linens on the bed, and a listening ear for any problems we may need to discuss. Like Apollos, she is a friend who is "a great help." I hope my life can be characterized as a great help to others. I do not know how to cook a pot roast, I am not the greatest host, and sometimes I talk more than I listen. However, I am convinced that God can teach each of us how to use our gifts and talents to be a great help to those He leads across our pathway.

6. Before Priscilla and Aquila taught Apollos about Jesus, Apollos was familiar only with the teachings of John the Baptist. Look up Luke 3:16. What does John the Baptist say is a primary difference between himself and Jesus?

7. When Apollos went to the region of Achaia, he apparently went to the city of Corinth. He met some of the believers to whom Paul had ministered during his 18-month stay. In Paul's letter to the church in Corinth he expresses his appreciation for the work of Apollos. Read 1 Corinthians 3:5-9. What do you think Paul is trying to say?

8. Is there someone who always seems to be "a great help" to you? If so, include that person in a prayer of thanksgiving.

9. Is there something you can do today to be "a great help" to someone else?

MEMORY CHALLENGE

To assist with memorizing the Scripture reference, name five ways we can imitate the one God. Name five ways the one God shows His love to His children.

DAY FOUR

Love of God

Read Acts 19:1-12.

1. While Apollos was in Corinth, where was Paul?

2. What was the response to Paul the first time he was in Ephesus? (See Acts 18:19-21.)

Today the city of Ephesus is no longer a thriving metropolis but rather a small town with overgrown ruins. However, at the time of Paul's visit Ephesus was one of the most vibrant cities in Asia Minor. It was situated on the Aegean Sea about 40 miles from Smyrna. Among its many beautiful buildings was the temple of Diana, famous for being one of the Seven Wonders of the World. The temple took 220 years to build, was beautifully adorned with statues, and was surrounded by over 120 columns.[1]

When Paul arrived in Ephesus he found 12 men whom he discovered were deficient in their knowledge of Jesus, much like Apollos. Paul asked them, *Did you receive the Holy Spirit when you believed?* They answered, *No, we have not even heard that there is a Holy Spirit.* Paul began to teach them the way of God more accurately by teaching them the difference between John's baptism and that of Jesus. Paul now saw clearly why the Lord had sent him back to Ephesus.

3. Romans 10:14-15 may be Paul's explanation for his work in Ephesus. How do his comments relate to today's reading in Acts 19?

The 12 who heard Paul speak welcomed the truth, so he baptized them in the name of Jesus. When he laid his hands on them, they received the Holy Spirit and received the miraculous gift of different languages with which they taught others about Jesus.

My wife and I moved to California from Illinois when I enrolled in graduate school. The increase in housing costs was a shock to our small family budget. However, the cost of tuition at my school was even more overwhelming. After my first semester I had a professor ask if I was receiving the ministerial scholarship. I told him I did not even know such a scholarship existed. I went to the registrar's office and applied. They awarded me a 50-percent reduction in tuition for the remainder of my program.

That first semester I was doing my best to do everything I knew to do. Then someone told me there was more I could receive. I was thrilled. In the same way, some of the people in Ephesus were living in obedience to all the knowledge they had. However, all they knew was what they had learned from the teachings of John the Baptist. There was more to learn, and it was theirs for the asking. Their love of God helped them not only to see the truth of John's message but also to be open to the truth of salvation through Jesus and the free gift of the Holy Spirit.

Paul spoke boldly in the synagogue at Ephesus for three months. Eventually opposition surfaced. When it did, he left the synagogue and took the disciples with him to a convenient lecture hall where he continued his discussions for more than two years. God demonstrated His approval of Paul's ministry with extraordinary miracles.

4. How does Paul describe John's baptism? (See Acts 19:4.)

5. Repentance is a vital part of salvation. What do the following scriptures say about repentance?
   a. Isaiah 30:15

   b. Luke 5:32

   c. 2 Peter 3:9

   d. 1 John 1:9

6. All four Gospel writers agree on that with which Jesus would baptize His followers. Look up any of the following scriptures and indicate what the baptism is: Matthew 3:11, Mark 1:8, Luke 3:16, or John 1:33.

7. What are some of the functions of the Holy Spirit?
   a. John 14:26

b. John 16:7-8

c. John 16:13

d. Acts 1:8

8. How should we love the Lord? (See Mark 12:30.)

9. How do we show our love to the Lord? (See John 14:23.)

10. If the Holy Spirit empowers you (Acts 1:8) and you show your love to the Lord by being obedient to His commands (John 14:23), what area of your life could you ask the Holy Spirit to empower so that you might be more obedient?

MEMORY CHALLENGE

Post the Memory Challenge on your refrigerator, and say it aloud each time you open the door.

DAY FIVE

Love of Power

Read Acts 19:11-22.

1. Who was Sceva? (See Acts 19:14.)

2. What were his sons doing?

Paul's ministry in Ephesus was powerful. God demonstrated His approval of Paul's message by curing the sick and driving out evil spirits. Some Jews were also driving out evil spirits. Among them were the seven sons of the Jewish priest named Sceva. The method they used was to say, *In the name of Jesus, whom Paul preaches, I command you to come out.* Perhaps they had watched Paul and were fascinated by what he said and the results that followed. Maybe they tried to imitate him, not knowing it was the Holy Spirit who did the miracles through Paul.

People are often fascinated by spiritual issues. For some reason many people find the dark side of the spiritual world particularly intriguing. Both the prospect of a reality that is beyond our five senses and the power associated with such a realm can be intoxicating. Inappropriate use of power is one of Satan's great temptations. Satan told Eve she would be like God if she ate the forbidden fruit. Satan told Jesus he would give Him the kingdoms of the world if He would worship him. A more subtle temptation is to believe that a godly spiritual life can be lived apart from a relationship with the Giver of life.

The sons of Sceva apparently wanted the power they saw exhibited by Paul. When they tried to cast out an evil spirit *in the name of Jesus, whom Paul preaches*, the evil spirit answered them by saying he knew both Jesus and Paul, but he did not know them. Then the man in whom the evil spirit lived overpowered all seven men and brutally beat them. The news traveled quickly among the Jews and Greeks, causing them to reverence the name of Jesus, so much so that many who indulged in the secret sin of sorcery confessed and publicly burned the scrolls they used.

Dabbling in sorcery or the occult is neither innocent nor harmless. It is dangerous. Likewise, attempting to do righteous acts without being in a relationship with the Lord is also risky. The people of Ephesus saw the consequences of both. However, when relationship and obedience are combined, God is glorified, and His power is displayed (see Acts 19:20).

3. Read the following scriptures concerning evil practices. Summarize what you learn from them.

   a. Deuteronomy 18:9-14

   b. Isaiah 8:19

   c. Malachi 3:5

   d. Revelation 9:20-21

4. Which practices listed in the above scriptures have become so common that we give them little thought?

5. How do we protect ourselves from such practices?

6. In what ways does Satan tempt people today with power?

7. Describe a time when you have been hurt by someone else's abusive power.

8. Name a way in which you have some sort of power or control over another. Offer a prayer that you would stay in relationship with the ultimate Source of all power and not abuse what He has entrusted to you.

MEMORY CHALLENGE

Use the Memory Challenge in a prayer, asking God's help to do what it says.

DAY SIX

Love and Money

Read Acts 19:21-41.

1. What did the city clerk say the whole world knew about the city of Ephesus? (See Acts 19:35.)

2. What did the city clerk say fell from heaven? (See verse 35.)

Artemis was a goddess whose mythology brought together beliefs about the Roman goddess Diana and a fertility goddess whose origins were in Asia. Apparently a meteorite fell from the sky and was placed in the temple of Diana and was worshiped as an image of Artemis. Silversmiths depended on the trade of models and silver shrines of Artemis. This trade was affected negatively by the influence of the gospel message.[1]

Paul was making plans to go to Jerusalem and Rome. He sent Timothy and Erasmus on ahead while he stayed in Ephesus a little longer. He preached with such persuasive power that the entire city felt the impact, not only spiritually but economically. Throughout the whole province of Asia, the idol industry was suffering dramatic losses in both sales and profits, and he was blamed.

Demetrius, an Ephesian silversmith, made an emotional appeal to his fellow craftsmen. They were all feeling the financial pinch. He said the crisis they all were facing was because Paul preached against their gods. He was very conscious that belief determined behavior. Paul's persuasive words were changing the way people thought about idols, and this was a direct link to the suffering incomes of the craftsmen.

As Demetrius spoke, they began to see the problem. If Ephesians believed Paul, their businesses, jobs, incomes, economic security, the worship of their goddess, and the Temple would be undermined. The speech of Demetrius sparked a riot. They tried to find Paul but could not, so they seized his traveling companions, Gaius and Aristarchus. They dragged them to the public theater, which then became the scene of chaos and mass confusion.

Demetrius was probably far more offended that Paul's

preaching hurt his profits than he was by the content of Paul's assertion that *man-made gods are not gods at all.* Economics and religion will never be equal partners. The love of money will always see God as a means to an end, and the love of God will never tolerate the worship of any other. One must choose.

3. What did Jesus say is impossible in Matthew 6:24?

4. What was Jesus' admonition in Matthew 6:31-33?

5. Paul cautioned his good friend Timothy in 1 Timothy 6:9-10. Give an example of how Paul's caution is still relevant today.

6. Later in his journey, Paul would write a letter to the believers in the city of Ephesus. In it he gives instructions designed to help the believers in their Christian walk. Read Ephesians 5:1-21, and answer the questions below.

   a. Who are we to imitate? (See verse 1.)

   b. What kind of life are we to live? (See verse 2.)

   c. Of what should there not even be a hint? (See verses 3-4.)

   d. How is an idolater described? (See verse 5.)

   e. What kind of children are we to live like? (See verse 8.)

   f. What does the fruit of the light consist of? (See verse 9.)

   g. What should we find out? (See verse 10.)

   h. What makes everything visible? (See verse 14.)

MEMORY CHALLENGE

Ask a friend to check you on reciting Ephesians 4:29—5:1.

Acts

■ A Study of Acts 20:1—21:6

LESSON 16

DAY ONE

Whose Agenda?

Read Acts 20:1—21:6.

Paul's journeys took him to the towns and areas on the eastern side of the Mediterranean Sea (sometimes called the Great Sea). His travels are described as three missionary journeys, followed by his trip from Jerusalem to Rome as a prisoner. Many of the Bibles we use have maps in the back that show Paul's various trips. Acts chapter 20 describes a portion of Paul's third missionary journey. He decided to go to Jerusalem. He was in Ephesus, and the shortest route would be to head directly south. However, he preferred to take a path similar to his second trip, following the coastline of the Aegean Sea north, then west, then south down into Corinth (present-day Greece). This decision was recorded in Acts 19:21. From Corinth he would sail to Syria and then on to Jerusalem. If the Aegean Sea were the face of a clock and the numbers of the clock were coastal towns, it would be like traveling from 3 o'clock counterclockwise to 5 o'clock instead of simply going clockwise from 3 to 5. Apparently Paul wanted to revisit the people to whom he had ministered on previous trips before returning to Jerusalem.

Paul's plans did not work out as he intended, but certainly God's plans came to pass. In question 3 below you will find an alphabetical listing of the places Paul visited on his third missionary journey. Phrygia, Macedonia, Achaia, and Syria are areas in which many of the towns are found. This third trip actually begins in Antioch (Acts 18:23).

1. Where did Paul go from Antioch? (See Acts 18:23.)

2. What route did Paul take to Ephesus? (See Acts 19:1.)

3. Chapter 20 begins with Paul in Ephesus. Use the following verses to place the alphabetical list in the order that Paul went on his journey from Ephesus to Jerusalem. (See Acts 20:1-3, 6, 13-15; 21:1-3, 7-8, 17.)
   Assos
   Caesarea
   Chios (Kios)
   Cos
   Ephesus
   Greece (also called Achaia, which includes Corinth)
   Jerusalem
   Macedonia (first time)
   Macedonia (second time, including Philippi)
   Miletus
   Mitylene
   Patara
   Phoenicia
   Ptolemais
   Rhodes
   Samos
   Syria (and the town of Tyre)
   Troas

4. What was the last thing Paul did for the disciples in Ephesus before leaving them? (See Acts 20:1.)

MEMORY CHALLENGE

Ephesians 5:2

Live a life of love, just as Christ loved us and gave himself up for us as a fragrant offering and sacrifice to God.

5. As Paul traveled through Macedonia to Greece, what did he do? (See 20:2.)

6. Paul had learned that an important part of nurturing people in the faith is encouragement. He may have learned this from the Holy Spirit, from his own experience, and from others. There is a strong likelihood that he also learned this practice from a traveling companion who accompanied him on the first missionary journey. Who would that person be? (Hint: see Acts 4:36.)

7. Instead of sailing from Greece to Syria, as Paul had planned, he and his companions traveled back through Macedonia. Why did he change his plans? (See Acts 20:3.)

A winter blizzard recently descended on the northeastern coast of the United States. Portions of New England were hit with over two feet of snow in 24 hours. The kids celebrated the closing of schools while travelers bemoaned the cancellation of flights at all the major airports. Frustrations abound when travel plans are messed up. All of us have watched people at airports, hotels, or on the road who have become irate because their travel arrangements did not work out as they had planned. Ticket agents, desk clerks, and innocent bystanders become villains, and everyone is a potential object of the frustrated traveler's wrath. I must admit that there have been times when my traveling agenda has been thrown off and my response has been less than stellar. I wish I were less aware of my own agenda and more aware of God's agenda.

Paul wanted to be in Jerusalem by the celebration of Pentecost. Yet with each change of plans, he looked for opportunities to talk about Christ, break bread with fellow believers, and be an encouragement. God's agenda was his agenda.

8. Describe a time when you became frustrated over a change of plans (such as travel plans, family plans, or career plans).

9. Why is it so difficult to consider what God might do in the midst of frustrated plans?

DAY TWO

Whose Reputation?

Read Acts 20:1-12.

1. How long was Paul in Greece?

2. Paul's letter to the Romans was apparently completed near the end of his three-month stay in Greece (also called Achaia). Read Romans 15:25-26. What had the people of Macedonia and Greece done?

3. Paul was traveling to Jerusalem and taking with him a significant sum of money and other valuables. He also took along a number of traveling companions. Who were they? (See Acts 20:4.)

4. Based on the pronouns used in verses 5-6, who else was accompanying Paul?

These men certainly would have provided additional security for Paul. The valuable offering could be carried by several different people. Or if it was carried by one person, there would still be less likelihood of being robbed, because they were traveling in a larger group.

Security from thieves is not the only issue. The group of travelers also provides accountability for Paul. He was aware that there are temptations when dealing with money. The fellow travelers provided a "safety zone" for Paul, because temptation is more likely to take root when a person feels his or her actions will not be discovered. We do not know if Paul would be tempted in the proper handling of the offering, but their presence prevented temptation from finding any fertile ground to grow. The Body of Believers is intended to hold the members of the Body accountable. When we separate ourselves, we become more susceptible to particular types of temptation.

Finally, the traveling companions provided a protection for the reputation of both Paul and the Church. Some of them probably came from the very churches that had provided the offering. They could report back to their own people not only the way in which the gifts were handled but also the joy experienced by those who received the gifts in Jerusalem.

God's protection of the integrity of His people was not limited to finances. His protection can also be seen in the story of the healing of the young man who fell out of the window during Paul's long-winded talk. He fell three stories and was pronounced dead. Paul knew death was powerless before God. He threw his arms around the boy's broken body and said, *He's alive!* Skeptics might minimize the miracle by saying the boy never died in the first place. However, the person writing the account, who was also an eyewitness of the event, was Luke, a physician. He certainly gives creditability to the authenticity of the events. Once again we can see that God can use other people to provide protection, accountability, and credibility if we will allow Him to.

5. Paul warned his friend Timothy about the temptation of money. Read 1 Timothy 6:9-10. What has happened to some who have been eager for money?

6. Paul told the people in Corinth that God helps us with temptation. In 1 Corinthians 10:12-13, what did Paul say God will do for us?

7. Can you think of a time when God used someone else to protect you, your reputation, or your integrity? Write a specific instance below.

8. Are you facing any temptations now that you would be willing to share with a group?

9. How could God use the Body of Believers to help you avoid being trapped by temptation?

MEMORY CHALLENGE

Try to sing the Memory Challenge to the tune of "The Battle Hymn of the Republic."

DAY THREE

Whose Harvest?

Read Acts 20:13-16.

1. *a.* How did Paul get to Assos?

   b. How did the rest of the group get to Assos?

2. This scene is very similar to what Jesus did in Mark 6:45-46. Read those verses, and record what Jesus did after the people left Him.

Everyone, including Luke, in Troas boarded a ship sailing for Assos, but Paul decided to walk the 30 miles alone. Maybe his life had gotten so crowded with people and problems that he had to find time to be alone with God. Our spiritual health is dependent upon finding time to be with our Creator.

3. Why was Paul in a hurry to reach Jerusalem? (See Acts 20:16.)

4. After God used Moses to bring the Hebrew people out of Egyptian bondage, he instituted several holidays or feasts. These were times of sacred assembly when the people could come together to honor God and celebrate His blessings. When Paul left Philippi, the people had just finished celebrating which feast? (See Acts 20:6.)

5. Look up Leviticus 23:4-6.

   a. On what calendar day did the Feast of Unleavened Bread begin?

   b. The Feast of Unleavened Bread immediately follows which significant holiday?

Passover marks the time when the Lord's angel passed over every home in Egypt that had blood on the doorframe (Exodus 12:7) but took the life of the firstborn of every home that did not have blood on it. The Hebrew people were spared from the terrible plaque, and as a result Pharaoh told the enslaved Hebrews to leave Egypt. The Feast of Unleavened Bread celebrates God's provision for the people, both in protecting them from the Egyptians when Pharaoh changed his mind and for the manna and quail He provided for their sustenance in the desert.

6. The reason for eating unleavened bread for seven days is explained in Deuteronomy 16:3. Write the reason below.

The Feast of Weeks (also called Pentecost) was a celebration of the harvest and God's bountiful blessings. Each year the very first grain that was harvested was to be brought to the priest and offered to the Lord on the day after the Sabbath of the week it was harvested. Seven weeks later the harvest would be complete, and the people would celebrate. This was the Feast of Weeks. The name "Pentecost" comes from the fact that 50 days passed from the harvesting of the first grain to the time of the celebration.

7. What were the people to do as part of the celebration of the Feast of Weeks? (See Deuteronomy 16:10.)

8. What were the people *not* to do in regard to the harvest (Leviticus 23:22), and why were they not to do it?

When I was a little boy, our grade-school PTA had a Christmas sale. My parents took me to the school on a Saturday. The gym had been set up with items that we could purchase as Christmas gifts. My dad had given me some money, and I bought him a wonderful shoe shine kit that his PTA dues had probably already paid for in the first place. However, I now had the joy of watching my dad unwrap the gift and shower me with gratitude on Christmas morning. I did not have any of my own money. It was all Dad's anyway. I got to buy my dad a gift, but it was only because he had provided the resources for me in the first place.

In the same way, we may bring a tithe or an offering to God, but it is not as if we are giving Him "His portion." It all belongs to Him. All we have is ours simply because of His blessing. What we give should be in proportion to the blessings we have received and should be done in a way that also helps to care for the poor and the disenfranchised.

9\. *a.* What feast was being celebrated during the time that Jesus was crucified? (Hint: see Matthew 26:17.)

b. Based on what you have learned, how do Jesus' death and His words in Matthew 26:26-28 relate to the celebration of Passover and the Feast of Unleavened Bread?

10\. What feast was being celebrated when the Holy Spirit first came upon the believers in Jerusalem? (See Acts 2:1.)

How many were baptized on that day? (See Acts 2:41.)

Based on what you have learned, how does what happened on that day relate to the Feast of Weeks?

MEMORY CHALLENGE

How should you live your life?

DAY FOUR

Whose Love?

Read Acts 20:17-38.

1. Paul had decided to sail past Ephesus. He was in a hurry to reach Jerusalem and was trying to avoid spending time in the province of Asia. He had stopped in Miletus, which was about 20 miles south of Ephesus. Whom did Paul ask to join him in Miletus? (See Acts 20:17.)

2. What was Paul's message to both the Jews and the Greeks? (See verse 21.)

3. What was the task the Lord had given him? (See verse 24.)

4. What did Paul proclaim? (See verse 27.)

This was a tender scene. The elders in Ephesus had become trusted friends. Paul's preaching had laid the groundwork for their salvation. His teaching had played a role in their growth, and their mutual hospitality had been a means of grace that cemented their relationship.

Paul was giving a farewell message. Somehow he was aware that he would never see them again. He understood the cost of continued obedience to Christ. He found it difficult to say good-bye to the ones the Lord had given into his care. He remembered the excitement of watching them repent and turn in faith to Jesus. He had watched their spiritual birth and rejoiced over their daily growth. However, they did not belong to Paul. They never did. They belonged to Christ.

When my children or friends face difficult circumstances or painful events, I am often frustrated because I cannot fix the problem, control the circumstances, or alleviate the pain. In those moments I need to be reminded that God loves my children more than I do (as inconceivable as that may seem), cares about my friends more than I ever will, and knows how to watch over all of them better than I ever could. They belong to God, and He is trustworthy.

Paul dearly loved the friends from Ephesus. He would willingly lay down his life for them, but now he had to simply trust them to the Lord's care. He took advantage of the last few minutes he would have with them to share important things that he did not want them to forget. He reminded them of their responsibilities and warned them of the dangers ahead.

5. What are the two *instructions* Paul gave to the Ephesian elders? (See Acts 20:28.)

6. What are the two *warnings* Paul gave to the Ephesian elders? (See verses 29-30.)

7. What are the two ways Paul *committed* the Ephesian elders? (See verse 32.)

8. What are the *words* of Jesus that Paul quoted (See verse 35.)

9. What did Paul do for the elders before he departed? (See verse 36.)

10. Luke did not record Paul's prayer, but a prayer for the Ephesians offered by Paul is found in the third chapter of the Book of Ephesians. It reveals Paul's tender love for them. Read Ephesians 3:14-21, and put in your own words how Paul described the love of Christ.

MEMORY CHALLENGE

Ask God's help in overcoming the barriers to living according to the memory verse.

DAY FIVE

Whose Race?

Read Acts 20:22-24.

1. What did Paul anticipate in every city he visited? (See verse 23.)

2. Who gave Paul his assignment? (See verse 24.)

Paul's task was to testify to the gospel of God's grace. That was the driving force behind all his travels. He had been redeemed by Christ on the road to Damascus, he had been set apart by the Holy Spirit, he had been commissioned by the elders in a prayer in Antioch, and he had been confirmed by the fruit of his labor in the many towns he visited. His life and labor were a witness to God's love and grace.

Several themes and images run throughout Paul's speech and writings. One image is found in today's reading. He called his ministry a race and said that the one thing that can give his life meaning is to finish the race.

One of my all-time favorite runners is Jim Ryan. He was the world record-holder in the mile and was an American hero when I was a boy. I remember watching the 1972 Olympics in Munich, Germany, in which he was to run against the best in the world. The race was basically four laps around the track (1,500 meters) and lasted less than four minutes. In the qualifying heat I watched as Jim kept pace with the other runners. He was part of the pack, but that was OK, because he had a great kick and was in excellent position to win the race and move on to the finals. As the runners came around the curve at the end of the third lap, a runner stepped on Jim and caused him to fall. I was stunned. He looked injured. The race was over for him. There was no way he could recover. However, he picked himself off the ground and started limping around the track. He had gone to the Olympics to finish the race, and that was exactly what he did. I cannot tell you who won that race, but I continue to be inspired by the one who was determined to finish the race.

Let's look at some of the other ways Paul uses this imagery to describe his spiritual journey.

3. In 1 Corinthians 9:24-27 Paul admonished the believers to have purpose, to be intentional, and not to be lazy in their efforts. Give an example of how a person's spiritual life would resemble "a man running aimlessly," or "a man shadowboxing."

4. In Galatians 5:7 Paul uses the running metaphor to confront the believers. What would be an example in your spiritual journey of what Paul describes in that verse?

5. Read Philippians 3:12-14. Paul admonishes the believers to be determined and persistent.

   a. In order to reach his goal, what does Paul forget?

   b. What might this include?

   c. To what does Paul strain?

6. We do not know who wrote the Book of Hebrews, but the author uses the same type of imagery that Paul uses. Read the inspiring passage found in Hebrews 12:1-3.

   a. What should we throw off?

   b. How should we run?

   c. Where should we fix our eyes?

7. When Paul wrote his second letter to Timothy, he had finished all his missionary trips and was standing trial in Rome. He apparently knew that he had done all Christ had asked him to do. What statement did he make in 2 Timothy 4:7 that summarized his obedience to God's call?

8. As you pray concerning your own spiritual journey, try using the imagery of running.

MEMORY CHALLENGE

Each time the phone rings, try to recite the Memory Challenge before you answer the call.

DAY SIX

Whose Family?

Read Acts 21:1-6.

1. Where did the ship on which Paul and his companions were riding unload its cargo?

2. How long did they stay in that town?

3. With whom did they stay?

4. After praying with Paul and his companions on the beach, to where did the disciples of Tyre and their families return?

Paul had been to many towns sharing the Good News. His traveling companions had accompanied Paul on much of this third missionary journey. Paul's life must have seemed dangerous to some and exciting to others. Because of the focus on his travels, it is easy to miss the significance of the final statement concerning the believers in Tyre. The Scripture record simply says, *They returned home.* The home is where true discipleship is lived out. It can simultaneously be the easiest place and the hardest place to exhibit the fruit of the Spirit.

Whether you live in a family of believers or are the only believer, whether you are a part of a large blended family or live alone, whether you have material wealth or very little, your home is the screen on which your discipleship is displayed. Compassion begins at home. Lessons in forgiveness abound with family members. Principles of sharing, encouragement, kindness, and patience mean very little outside the home if they are not practiced inside the home. Paul wrote, *[Love] keeps no record of wrongs* (1 Corinthians 13:5). Some might conclude from Paul's statement that he must have had no siblings! But in reality he simply indicated the standard of behavior Christ expects.

5. Jesus healed a man who was demon-possessed and lived in the tombs in the region of the Gerasenes. After he had been healed, the man wanted to accompany Jesus. Read Luke 8:38-39. Where did Jesus tell the man to go, and what did He tell him to do?

6. Paul taught Timothy that religion or piety begins in the home. Use 1 Timothy 5:1-4 to answer the following questions.

   How should we treat the elderly?

   How should we treat younger men and women?

   How should children and grandchildren put their religion into practice?

7. Read 1 Corinthians 13:4-7. Which characteristic of love is sometimes difficult to live out in your home?

   Which characteristic of love would you like to be known for this week?

Our discipleship is not measured by the decision or lifestyles of our family members. Everyone has the freedom to make his or her own choices, including our family members. However, our discipleship can be measured by the way in which we respond to our family. We are called to be vehicles of love and grace. We usually do not need to travel overseas to be a messenger of the Good News. We may do more good by simply going to the room down the hall.

MEMORY CHALLENGE

Write from memory Ephesians 4:29—5:2.

Acts

■ A Study of Acts 21:7—22:2

LESSON 17

DAY ONE

Enemies or Friends?

Read Acts 21:7-40, focusing on verses 7-9.

1. Where were the final two stops before Paul reached Jerusalem?

2. How did Luke describe Philip?

At each port Paul and his companions made contact with Christians who poured out love and affection. Many begged him not to go on to Jerusalem.

The last stop before arriving in Jerusalem was in Caesarea, the capital of Palestine. Paul and his companions would walk the rest of the way, but first they went to see Philip, who invited them to stay at his house. Paul's friends were probably thrilled to meet their host, the first Christian missionary to share the gospel with the Samaritans. Maybe Philip told his guests how the Lord led him to the Ethiopian eunuch on the road to Gaza over 20 years earlier. The stories shared by these believers may have actually helped Luke create a more accurate record for his history of the Early Church.

If one only reads portions of Acts at each sitting, it is easy to miss the drama and significance of this situation. The recipient of Luke's writings is Theophilus. He may have read the book in one sitting and would have recognized the name of Philip as a character mentioned earlier in the story.

Philip was one of the seven, elected by the disciples to oversee the distribution of food. Stephen was another one of the seven. By virtue of their work and shared experiences, Philip and Stephen were likely close comrades.

Stephen became the first martyr of the new group of Jewish believers (see Acts 7:58). Standing there giving approval to Stephen's death was Paul (at the time named Saul). Therefore, the scene in Acts 21 is a mark of God's great grace in the hearts and lives of His children. Philip welcomed into his home and extended warm hospitality to a man who consented to the killing of his friend and fellow worker, Stephen. In fact, Stephen's death was the start of bitter opposition to the believers in Jerusalem, which probably caused Philip and his family to leave that city. However, the power of God's grace can dissolve bitterness, melt away resentment, turn anger into forgiveness, and transform enemies into friends.

3. Can you name two brothers from the Old Testament whose treatment of each other led to anger and mistrust, but God's work in their lives led to a wonderful reunion? (See Genesis 25:34; 27:41; 33:4.)

MEMORY CHALLENGE

1 John 1:5

This is the message we have heard from him and declare to you: God is light; in him there is no darkness at all.

4. Can you name another group of brothers whose jealousy caused them to contemplate murder, but through God's grace they reconciled and prospered? (See Genesis 37:11, 20-21; 45:15.)

5. Are there any among your current friends with whom your first contact was strained, difficult, or painful? If so, how did God bring about reconciliation?

DAY TWO

Ignorance or Knowledge?

Read Acts 21:10-16.

1. From where did Agabus come? (See verse 10.)

2. In what city did Paul first meet Agabus? (See Acts 11:27.)

Paul had been brought to Antioch by Barnabas. Shortly thereafter, he met Agabus. At that time Agabus prophesied that a severe famine would spread over the entire world. The prophecy came to pass. In fact, the impact of the famine on believers in Jerusalem was one reason Paul's companions were with him. They were bringing money they had collected to give to church leaders for distribution.

Agabus came to see Paul and was led by the Spirit to give Paul a message. The group that was there watched Agabus dramatize the prophecy that the Jews would bind Paul and hand him over to the Gentiles. When the group realized what Agabus was foretelling, they pleaded with Paul not to go to Jerusalem. Maybe they thought they were helping, but Paul said they were breaking his heart and making obedience more difficult.

A few years ago on television was a show whose weekly plot centered around a man in Chicago who received the daily newspaper a day early. In other words, he knew the next day's headlines before the events actually happened. Each week the main character would try to help others avoid accidents, avert disasters, or stop crimes. I once asked a Sunday School class what they would like to know if they could know it a day early. Some jokingly said they would like to know the winning lottery number. Others said they would like to know accidents, illnesses, or dates of death ahead of time. However, many said they did not want to know anything ahead of time.

Sometimes a little knowledge can produce more anxiety than blind trust. The disciples were concerned about what would happen to Paul. Paul was concerned only about being obedient to Christ. Trust does not deny the fact—it simply acknowledges the One who controls the fact.

3. Who pleaded with Paul not to go to Jerusalem? (See Acts 21:12.)

4. What was Paul prepared to do? (See verse 13.)

5. Where did Paul stay in Jerusalem? (See verse 15-16.)

6. Is there anything you would like to know ahead of time?

7. What are some ways in which God may be merciful in *not* letting us know what the future holds?

8. What are some things God has already told us about the future?

MEMORY CHALLENGE

Write the Memory Challenge on a card, and post it on your mirror.

DAY THREE

Peter or Paul

Read Acts 21:17-19.

1. What did Paul report?

The author of Acts, Luke, did not record any of the details of Paul's report. He seemed to have no need to document the authenticity of Paul's apostleship, probably because he had spent the previous eight chapters chronicling Paul's ministry. Many of the details that Paul shared with the elders are likely the same details that Luke had already written for the benefit of Theophilus and those of us after Theophilus who read the Book of Acts.

Luke had given particular attention to two key leaders of the Early Church, Peter and Paul. He wrote about the ministry of the former in chapters 1 through 12. Luke also recorded Peter's speech at the Council in Jerusalem (chapter 15), but he made no reference to him after that time. Beginning in chapter 13, Luke traced the ministry of Paul, and the fruit of his ministry was so evident that Luke apparently found no need to substantiate Paul's ministry by reporting the details again.

The stories Luke chose to include in the biographical sketches of Peter and Paul are amazingly similar. Listed below are some of those similarities.

2. Refer to the references to answer the questions regarding Peter and Paul.

Luke records their first Gentile converts.

Peter's first was named ___________ (Acts 10:24, 44).

Paul's first was named ___________ (Acts 13:7, 12).

Luke records their first sermons.

The location of Peter's was ___________ (Acts 1:12; 2:14).

The location of Paul's was ___________ (Acts 13:14, 16).

Luke tells how each man had a confrontation with a magician.

Peter's confrontation was with a man named ___________ (Acts 8:9-23).

Paul's confrontation was with a man named ___________ (Acts 13:8-11).

Luke tells how through each of them God healed a man who was lame from birth.

Peter's healing took place in what part of the city of Jerusalem? __________ (Acts 3:1)

Paul's healing took place in the city of __________ (Acts 14:8).

Luke tells how both were physically persecuted.

Who was responsible for Peter's flogging? __________ (Acts 5:40-41)

Who was responsible for Paul's stoning? __________ (Acts 14:19)

Luke shows how both men were led by a vision to take the gospel to a new group of people.

Peter had his vision at what time of day? __________ (Acts 10:9)

Paul had his vision during the __________ (Acts 16:9).

Luke reports how both were imprisoned and miraculously released.

Upon his release, Peter went to the house of __________ (Acts 12:12).

During his imprisonment, Paul went to the house of __________ (Acts 16:34).

Luke shows that through their ministry the Holy Spirit was imparted to believers.

For Peter this happened with the household of __________ (Acts 10:24, 44).

For Paul this happened with the 12 believers in the town of __________ (Acts 19:1, 6-7).

Luke records that some believed in the power of Peter's shadow and Paul's handkerchief.

For Peter, this took place in the city of __________ (Acts 5:15-16).

For Paul, this took place in the city of __________ (Acts 19:1, 12).

Luke tells how each of these men raised someone from the dead.

The name of the person Peter raised is __________ (Acts 9:40-41).

The name of the person Paul raised is __________ (Acts 20:10).

There are other similarities the reader can draw from the writings of Luke. The point is that Luke clearly established the spiritual authority of these two men. Paul needed no human defense before the Jerusalem council, just as Peter would need no defense. Their validity had been established by the work of the Holy Spirit in their lives.

3. Though it may not be as dramatic as the evidence of the Holy Spirit in the life of Peter and Paul, God does provide evidence of His work in the life of every believer. What is evidence of His work in your life?

MEMORY CHALLENGE

For whose life can you pray that God's light will dispel the darkness? Offer a prayer for that person.

DAY FOUR

The Law or Jesus?

Read Acts 21:17-25.

1. Who did Paul and his companions see the day after arriving in Jerusalem?

2. Earlier in Paul's journey, he met with the council at Jerusalem (Acts 15:13-14, 19-20). Who led that council, and what was the final judgment?

Paul was aware of the prophecy that the Jews of Jerusalem would find him and turn him over to the Gentiles. However, he must have anticipated that his brothers in Christ would give him a warm welcome. The problem was that James had already heard complaints about Paul. Jews from the provinces where Paul had been ministering had made their way to Jerusalem for the celebration for the Feast of Weeks. Many, angry at Paul for his work with the Gentiles, had already circulated rumors about him. James appeared to have anticipated Paul's visit and had a plan in mind to help mediate what he saw as a potentially explosive situation.

Paul gave the elders a detailed report of his work. He probably talked about the converts, the miracles, the growth of the believers, and the generous gift the Gentiles had sent to the needy in Jerusalem and Judea. The listeners praised God but then changed the subject to their pressing agenda.

The complaints were that Paul was telling the Jews who lived among the Gentiles to turn away from Moses, not to circumcise their children, and not to live according to the Jewish customs. These were serious charges. However, nothing in the sacred record of Scriptures indicates that Paul was demanding this behavior of the Jews who lived among the Gentiles.

James proclaimed that thousands of Jews had become believers and that all of them remained zealous for the law. Jesus was somehow incorporated into the keeping of the law instead of being the complete fulfillment of the law. Many people today believe that Jesus was a good man, or that He was one of the great prophets, or that He was a divinely inspired teacher. Accommodating Jesus into one's life is very different than surrendering his or her life to Him. Paul did not say that the Jews could not follow the law—he was simply saying what Jesus said, that the law would not bring reconciliation with God.

3. Prior to his visit to Jerusalem, Paul had written his letter to the Romans. It is as if God had prepared him for this very confrontation. What words did Paul use to describe the law in Romans 7:12, 14?

4. Paul believed that Christ frees us to live in a new way. What is that new way? (See Romans 7:6.)

5. What does Romans 8:3 mean to you?

6. Read Matthew 26:63-64. What does Jesus claim about himself?

7. Read John 14:6. What else does Jesus claim about himself?

8. Do you have any friends or acquaintances who believe Jesus was simply a good man, or any who believe that Jesus is just one of many ways to salvation?

9. What are some ways in which your words may indicate you believe in Jesus, but your actions indicate that He is not Lord of your life?

MEMORY CHALLENGE

What is the message we have heard?

DAY FIVE

Questions or Excuses?

Read Acts 21:26-36.

1. Why did Paul go to the Temple? (See Acts 21:26.)

2. Based on the description of the purification and offering mentioned in this chapter, Paul and the other men had taken a Nazarite vow. Look up Numbers 6:1-2. What type of vow is a Nazarite vow?

The Nazarite vow was a Jewish practice indicating a sense of gratitude for God's mercy. Paul was willing to abide by the request of the church elders, participate in the vow, pay for the animal sacrifices that were made at the completion of the purification day, and hopefully dispel the rumors that he had denounced Judaism. Before he could complete his vow, Jews from Asia spotted him in the Temple. They quickly spread this information, and their words impacted the city like a firebomb. Apparently no one tried to determine if the accusations against Paul were true. Religious hatred is never overly concerned about the truth of a matter when it finds a way to get even with the object of its hatred. So before Paul could respond, the crowd rushed him and dragged him out of the Temple area. They wanted him dead.

I once was asked to visit an elderly man with whom a mutual friend had tried to share the good news of the gospel—but he had questions that my friend could not answer. Upon my visit I was asked one of the questions that had been asked previously of my friend. I spent about 10 minutes providing an explanation. When I had finished, the gentleman responded as if my words had gone in one ear and out the other. He asked exactly the same question again. Now, it is possible that my response was terribly inadequate. However, I really believe that the gentleman was not looking for an answer but instead was using the question as an excuse to avoid making a decision about Christ. Often we do not want answers but rather want excuses for our attitudes and justification for our behavior. This was certainly true of the Jewish mob that took Paul.

A garrison of Roman soldiers was quartered nearby in the fortress of Antonia. When news reached them that the whole city was in an uproar, they rushed down the stairs to the angry crowd.[1] The show of Roman force was enough to make them stop beating Paul. Because the Roman commander could not make any sense out of what the people were saying, he arrested Paul, put him in chains, and ordered his men to take him to the barracks.

3. What did the soldiers do to keep Paul away from the violence of the angry crowd? (See Acts 21:35.)

4. Certain phrases of the 23rd psalm seem written for Paul for this very moment. Which statements of that psalm do you think relate?

5. What was the false assumption the people made about Paul that added to their frenzied anger? (See verse 29.)

6. It is easy to jump to conclusions without adequate evidence to support the conclusion. Satan often uses this method to deceive. Write a definition for the words "assume" and "presume."

7. Describe a time when you were not looking for an answer or explanation but rather were looking for an excuse to justify your attitudes or behavior.

MEMORY CHALLENGE

Read the Memory Challenge aloud three times, and then try to recite it from memory.

DAY SIX

Greek or Aramaic?

Read Acts 21:37—22:2.

1. What do the following scriptures say Paul would experience at Jerusalem?

   Acts 20:23

   Acts 21:11

2. How do the following scriptures confirm that what James asked of Paul (to take a Nazarite vow) was a good request and consistent with Jesus' teaching?

   Matthew 5:9

   John 14:27

   Romans 12:17-18

   James 3:18

3. How does 1 Peter 3:8-16 show that Paul's behavior was consistent with Christian principles in both doing what James requested and also speaking before the angry crowd? Explain your answer, and give the verses that support your conclusions.

Paul was willing to comply with James's request that he go through the process of ceremonial cleansing. This way, he would prove to the Jews from Asia that charges against him were unfounded. He wanted to work in harmony with his Christian brothers. James and the others wanted to avoid conflict, but the Lord had shown Paul that conflict was unavoidable. Paul knew that being in Jerusalem meant persecution.

4. Who did the commander think Paul was?

5. How did Paul describe Tarsus?

6. How does 1 Corinthians 14:18-19 relate to what Paul did with the Roman commander and the assembled Jews?

Before Paul could complete his vow, he was accosted by a violent mob. Roman soldiers rescued him from them and took him into custody. Just as he was being carried into the barracks, he decided that it was an ideal time to speak with his accusers about Jesus. He asked the commander, in flawless Greek, for permission to speak. This man had already jumped to the conclusion that Paul was an Egyptian terrorist leader, so when Paul spoke to him in his mother tongue, he was shocked. After Paul explained who he was, the commander granted him permission to speak.

Turning to the crowd, Paul made his characteristic gesture for silence. A hush fell, and then Paul began speaking in the common language of the Middle East, Aramaic. This was a kindred language to Hebrew, the language of scholarship and religion. Paul could speak Hebrew, and had he chosen to do so, some in the crowd would have understood him. But Paul was not interested in impressing them with his knowledge of languages. He wanted to capture their hearts. He believed this could be best accomplished by speaking in the marketplace language of the people. Probably the person most impressed with Paul's language skills was the commander. He was amazed that this prisoner could move so easily from Greek to Aramaic. Even though he probably could not understand Aramaic, he must have been intrigued with the effect Paul's words had on the audience.

Speaking in someone else's language can be very endearing. We take a large group of people every Christmas holiday on a Work and Witness trip to Mexico. Most of the people on the trip do not speak Spanish, and many of the Mexican nationals do not speak English. It is fun to watch the efforts at communication.

Sometimes we face problems in relationships because we think that since we speak the same language, we are communicating. This is a poor assumption. For many couples, one person will have a decision-making process that is based primarily on logic while his or her spouse has a decision-making process based on intuition. They may discuss the issues in English, but they are speaking two different "languages."

My youngest daughter loves to talk about dolls. My oldest daughter loves to wakeboard. My wife enjoys color and fabrics. None of these topics are natural "languages" for me. But effective family communication requires that I learn their "marketplace" language. It is key to understanding and appreciation.

7. Give an example from your experience of when knowing another language would have been beneficial.

MEMORY CHALLENGE

Ask a family member to listen to you recite the Memory Challenge.

Wisdom of the Word **Bible Study Series**

Acts

■ A Study of Acts 22—23

LESSON 18

DAY ONE

Words of Testimony

Read Acts 22 and 23, focusing on verses 1-16.

1. Where was Paul born?

2. Where was Paul raised?

3. Who was Paul's teacher?

The days of Paul's Nazarite vow were nearly over when the people of the city stormed the Temple and drug Paul outside the gates to kill him. Roman soldiers rescued Paul from the violent crowd but arrested him, because he was at the center of the chaos. Before being taken into the barracks, Paul asked for the opportunity to speak to the crowd.

Paul summarized his background. In his opening statement he established his credibility by identifying his origin, his faith, his heritage, his training, and his authority. He explained that he was trained by Gamaliel, one of the greatest teachers of the day. He also was once an authorized agent of the Sanhedrin, commissioned to stamp out Christianity. Paul knew these facts would lay the foundation for the rest of his, and the Lord's, story.

As Paul witnessed to the angry crowd, he quickly got to the part when his life had been transformed. He told them of his encounter with the risen Christ, which took place at high noon while he was on assignment to destroy the followers of Jesus. The intense light that blinded and knocked him down was the presence of God. The person who spoke to him was Jesus. He told him to go to Damascus, where he would receive further instructions. On that very day Paul began to walk by faith in Jesus Christ: blind, shattered, and humbled. In his zeal to destroy Jesus' followers, he discovered he had really been fighting against the God he honored. Paul wanted his audience to understand that he, too, had been deceived just as they were being deceived that very hour. He understood their struggle with sin and with the message he was preaching. He had been there himself.

Paul's experience on the Damascus road had been intense and powerful. He had heard the voice of Jesus, been blessed by an honorable Jewish-Christian brother, and been told he would be God's witness. He was now trusting the Holy Spirit to confront this crowd with the very things that exposed the deception in his own life: the light and power of His presence and the truth of His Word.

4. Ananias was the person through whom the Holy Spirit restored Paul's sight. To whom did Ananias say Paul would be a witness? (See Acts 22:15.)

   About what was Paul to witness?

MEMORY CHALLENGE

1 John 1:6

If we claim to have fellowship with him yet walk in the darkness, we lie and do not live by the truth.

Are we called to do the same?

5. On the steps of the barracks, Paul was simply sharing his faith by telling the crowd about his experience with Jesus. Witnessing is nothing more than that—simply telling someone about your experience with Jesus. Paul was prepared with his story. Are you? Below are some simple steps to help prepare you for sharing your faith.

   a. Just as Paul recited his history, write three sentences below that describe where you were born, where and by whom you were raised, and the circumstances that led to your first encounter with Jesus.

   b. If you know Christ as Savior, in four sentences describe what you experienced when you first met Him.

   c. Describe one or two key moments or events in your spiritual journey.

   d. Name one way in which you are still growing or learning.

   e. See if a member of your small group will allow you to practice telling your story. Work at keeping it brief. People who are interested (whose heart God has prepared) will ask you to share more.

   f. Ask God to open up an opportunity for you to share your faith, to calm your anxieties and fears, and to help you leave the "results" up to Him. If you have not yet accepted Christ as Savior, consider offering that prayer now, and ask your group to pray with you.

DAY TWO

Fighting Words

Read Acts 22:17-22.

1. In a previous visit of Paul to Jerusalem, why did the Lord tell him to leave the city?

2. What did Paul say was his attitude toward the stoning of Stephen?

3. Paul's comments about seeing a bright light, talking to Jesus, leaving Jerusalem, or stoning Stephen did not inflame the crowd. What was it that Paul said that caused the crowd to grow violent again?

The crowd listened as Paul told them what the Lord had revealed to him right there in Jerusalem several years before. Paul had returned from Arabia to Jerusalem to share the discoveries he had made in the Scriptures. He had found the prophecies of the ancient texts to be consistent with the fact that Jesus was the promised Messiah of God. He had expected the religious leaders to be as excited about the truth as he was. He had thought they would listen to him. It took a revelation from God to convince him that the leaders were not seeking truth but were trying to suppress it. So one day when he came to the Temple to pray, he fell into a trance and saw the Lord speaking to him, instructing him to leave Jerusalem because the people would not accept his testimony.

Surprisingly, this indictment of the Jews in Jerusalem did not enrage the listening crowd. What set them off was Paul's next claim, that the Lord had said, *I will send you far away to the Gentiles* (verse 21). Paul had hit their hot button. The term "Gentile" had become a "fighting word" in this gathering. Gentiles were unclean. Associating with a Gentile or visiting one was against Jewish law. Josephus, a Jewish historian, says that an inscription on the wall separating the court of the Israelites from the court of the Gentiles stated that "no stranger was permitted to come within the holy place on pain of death."

And now Paul was contending that God had rejected the Jews and had made the Gentiles His special people. This was unthinkable. The mob was ready to kill Paul.

Some words are so laden with emotional baggage that it becomes impossible to think clearly when those words or phrases are spoken. A few years into our marriage, my wife and I decided we would like to have children. Several years later, having had no success, we consulted a physician. The physician indicated there were reasons for our difficulties and suggested some medical procedures that might help my wife get pregnant. We did not want to pursue the suggested interventions. So for the next three years the subject of "motherhood" became more and more laden with emotion. The celebration of Mother's Day at church, a time to honor the wonderful love and work of mothers, became a time of dread, pain, and anger. We now have two wonderful children, but I doubt I will ever forget experiencing the emotions that can sometimes be attached to a simple word.

4. Some names are emotionally laden because of terrible racial prejudice. Read John 4:9. Based on that verse, what name of a group of people might engender prejudice and elicit feelings of anger or hurt in Paul's day?

   List some names or terms that you think may have the same effect in our culture.

5. Political issues can become so emotional and can so polarize people that it becomes nearly impossible to have a rational discussion about the issue. Name an issue for which you think this may be true.

6. Certain issues stir up great emotions within the Body of Believers. We will see an example of this in the next chapter. List some words or phrases that are difficult to discuss in the Church because they have become so volatile.

7. The worst break in communication can take place within the home. Are there words or topics that are completely avoided because of the feelings or prejudice associated with them? What are some of those issues?

8. Paul writes to the Corinthians about their divisions and lawsuits. Read the passages below, and write how his admonitions might help us deal with some of the topics listed above.

   1 Corinthians 3:18-19

   1 Corinthians 6:7-8

   2 Corinthians 6:11-13

MEMORY CHALLENGE

What can make us liars?

DAY THREE

Words of Citizenship

Read Acts 22:23-29.

1. What were the commander's orders?

2. Why was the commander alarmed?

When Paul said he had been sent by God to the Gentiles, the crowd exploded into another shouting frenzy. They were angry. They called for Paul's death. They threw dust into the air as a sign of their fury. They threw off their cloaks, probably as a sign that they were ready to stone Paul if the commander would just surrender him to their "justice."

The commander sent Paul to the barracks for a flogging in an attempt to restore order. He wanted to find out what Paul had done that angered them so much. He probably did not understand Paul's speech, because it was given in Aramaic. However, the commander was responsible for crowd control, and he certainly understood that the situation was explosive.

As the soldiers prepared to flog Paul, he calmly asked a centurion close by, *Is it legal for you to flog a Roman citizen who hasn't even been found guilty?* (verse 25). The centurion informed the commander, who then asked Paul to verify that he was a Roman citizen. When he said "Yes, I am," the commander knew he was in trouble. While trying to appease the emotional Jews, he had failed to care for his primary responsibility, to protect Roman citizens. He stopped the flogging immediately.

Paul was in a difficult position. The crowd outside wanted to beat him, while the soldiers inside were planning to flog him. The commander was in a difficult position. He could not release the prisoner because he had a duty to protect roman citizens and maintain order in Jerusalem. However, he could not bind (which he already had done) or flog a Roman citizen without a trial. Citizenship had its privileges, and Paul had the right to avail himself of all the benefits of citizenship.

3. How had the Roman commander obtained his Roman citizenship? (See Acts 22:28.)

4. How had Paul obtained his citizenship? (See verse 28.)

5. Later, in his letter to the Ephesians, Paul would use the imagery of citizenship to give them instructions. Read Ephesians 2:11-13.

   Whom did Paul describe as being excluded from citizenship, as foreigners to the covenants of promise, and without hope?

   What had now brought the Gentiles into the full privileges of the Kingdom?

6. According to Philippians 3:20, where is our citizenship?

7. Romans 8:15-17 describes how we become "citizens" or "heirs" of the kingdom of God. Just like Paul, we are "born" into citizenship. How do we know that we are children of the King?

8. Citizenship has both privileges and responsibilities.

   Name a privilege that comes with being a citizen of your home country.

   Name a responsibility that comes with being a citizen of your home country.

   Name a privilege that comes with being a citizen of the kingdom of God.

   Name a responsibility that comes with being a citizen of the kingdom of God.

MEMORY CHALLENGE

In your journal or the space below, write what the Memory Challenge means to you.

DAY FOUR

Words of Confidence

Read Acts 22:30—23:10

1. Who gave the order to have Paul struck on the mouth? (See Acts 23:2.)

2. We have met three men by the name of Ananias in Acts, referred to in the following scriptures. Distinguish between the three.

   Acts 5:1-2

   Acts 9:10

   Acts 23:2

3. Paul did not recognize the high priest, because he was not the high priest who had commissioned him to go to Damascus to put the Christians in prison. Who was the high priest in the following scriptures, and who was under investigation?

   John 11:45-49

   Acts 4:5-7

4. Which of the two men listed above is most likely to have been the high priest who gave Saul letters to bind believers in Damascus and take them to Jerusalem?

Paul was brought before the Sanhedrin so that the Roman commander might determine what the Jews were leveling their accusations against. Paul was not ashamed, because he had nothing to hide. His opening words brought a quick response from the high priest, who ordered those standing near Paul to strike him on the mouth. Paul was not timid in reacting to this misuse of power. What had just happened in the highest court of Judaism violated the law they were entrusted to uphold. It obviously angered Paul, because he said, *God will strike you, you white-washed wall!*

Paul did not know that the one who violated the law was the high priest himself. When he learned this, he apologized. Quick responses were characteristic of Paul. When he knew the Roman authorities had violated the law, he was quick to point it out; but when he realized he was also guilty, he was just as quick to apologize. He knew the Scriptures commanded respect for the high priest (Exodus 22:28).

This momentary diversion was not the reason the meeting was called, so Paul got right to the heart of the matter. He knew both Pharisees and Sadducees were present, and he knew the main issue that divided them: the resurrection of the dead. He quickly stated that he believed in the resurrection of the dead, and immediately the court was divided. A dispute broke out between the two factions. The Pharisees defended Paul. The debate was so intense that the commander was afraid for Paul's life, so he sent his troops to rescue Paul again.

Paul was confident in God, his faith, the foundational principles by which he lived. This type of confidence often intimates or infuriates those who are less confident, or those who have a need to control everyone else. Paul's confidence was in God and His revelation.

5. Read Matthew 26:59-66. Who else was treated as Paul was being treated by the high priest in the Sanhedrin? What did they do to Him? Did He tell the truth? Was He condemned for telling the truth?

6. What did Jesus say in Matthew 12:25 that applies to this situation and shows the fundamental weakness in the Sanhedrin?

7. On a scale of 1 to 10, with 1 being "no confidence" and 10 being "complete confidence," how confident are you in your Creator?

   How confident are you in the beliefs that you hold about your Creator?

   How confident would you be to share those beliefs before a group like the Sanhedrin?

   If you are willing, share your responses with your small group, and then ask God to help you in those areas where you lack confidence.

MEMORY CHALLENGE

Recite the Memory Challenge, using your own name in place of the pronoun "we."

DAY FIVE

Words of Comfort

Read Acts 23:11-22.

1. Who visited Paul in the night?

2. Paul was in Jerusalem. Where was he told he would go?

As Paul returned to the barracks, perhaps he wondered if the powerful men in the Sanhedrin (the Jewish ruling council) would ever repent and believe in Jesus. He must have grieved when he realized the extent to which corruption had influenced this part of Judaism. These men had been given opportunities to repent, but they persisted in doing wrong. What is worse is that they used religious authority to justify their actions. At one time in his life, Paul probably aspired to be part of this prestigious group, but on the road to Damascus he made a choice that changed his life forever. He exchanged those aspirations for Jesus Christ. It was a choice that changed Paul and changed the world.

Paul was once again in prison. He was being held by the Roman authorities. During the night the Lord visited him and comforted him. There was no condemnation about hasty words or any indication that the Lord was disappointed in him. Instead, he was commended for his testimony in Jerusalem and was told he would be given the opportunity to give his testimony in Rome. Paul may have wondered how he would get to Rome given his present circumstances. However, he had certainly learned to trust God's Word.

More than 40 men took an oath to kill Paul. They promised not to eat until their task was done. Their scheme required cooperation from the Sanhedrin and the chief priests in order to deceive the Roman officials. Neither Jewish law nor fairness was even considered. However, God's ability to protect His children from harm is powerful. Paul's nephew had learned about the plot and told Paul, so Paul sent his nephew to the commander. The commander must have already been uneasy about his role in mishandling this Roman citizen. He altered the plans for transporting Paul and thwarted the evil scheme.

3. Read Acts 19:21. Was this the first time Paul had intended to go to Rome?

4. What does the response of the chief priests and the elders tell us about their motives? (See Acts 23:20-21.)

   What did the group request that proves they were willing to deceive the other members of the Sanhedrin in order to kill Paul?

   Do you suppose that any members of the Sanhedrin defended Paul?

5. What words, events, or circumstances can be a discouragement to you in your journey of faith?

   What words, events, or circumstances can be a comfort in your journey of faith?

6. Is there someone in your life who could use some comfort? If so, consider sharing that person's circumstances with your small group, and include him or her in your time of prayer.

MEMORY CHALLENGE

Recite the Memory Challenge during each meal time.

DAY SIX

In My Own Words

Read Acts 23:23-35.

1. How many men accompanied Paul to Caesarea?

2. What was the name of the commander who wrote the letter?

3. To whom was the letter written?

The commander was grateful to Paul's nephew for advising him of the Jewish plot to ambush and kill Paul. He might have been deceived had he not heard this information. Now he could outwit the group and use the opportunity to impress the governor with his ability. He proceeded to detach nearly half the fortress garrison to ensure that Paul was given safe exodus from Jerusalem. He certainly did not want to explain to his superior the assassination plot against a Roman citizen who was in his charge.

The commander sent a large military escort to accompany Paul. He also wrote a letter to explain the situation, cleverly designed to give the facts of the situation while depicting the commander in the best possible light. To Governor Felix it would appear that everything had been handled properly and with Roman efficiency. No mention was made of Paul being in chains, nor of the flogging, nor of the embarrassing discovery of his citizenship. The commander made himself appear to be the hero of the hour.

4. Read the commander's letter. List some statements that are true.

List some statements that are partially true.

Are there any statements that are false?

5. Read Matthew 5:37. What instructions does Jesus give us about our witness and speaking the truth?

How do you think the Lord feels about embellishing the truth?

I have worked with many couples who struggle with conflict in their marriage relationship. Often a person will express his or her frustration or anger over a statement made by the spouse. The spouse will counter that he or she did not make that statement or did not make it in that way. Often conflicts arise over innuendo, body language, facial expression, or tone of voice. When called to account for such behavior, a person often pleads his or her innocence. He or she may repeat the statement back in a very innocent tone with no facial expression or inappropriate tone of voice. The person claims innocence. Fortunately we cannot get away with such behavior with God. He knows our hearts and our motives. He knows the truth. We must take responsibility not only for our words but also for our motives and attitudes as well. He cleanses us from the inside out so that our words become a reflection of our heart.

MEMORY CHALLENGE

Have a friend check you on reciting 1 John 1:5-6.

Acts

■ A Study of Acts 24—25

LESSON 19

DAY ONE

Flattery and Insults

Read Acts 24, focusing on verses 1-9.

1. Who brought charges against Paul?

2. How long had Paul been under guard in Caesarea before the group from Jerusalem arrived?

3. What do you think happened to the group of Jews mentioned in Acts 23:12?

Tertullus was a smooth talker. Ananias, the high priest, had brought the lawyer from Jerusalem to make formal charges against Paul. He used his verbal skills to win the favor of Governor Felix. His speech was filled with flattery more than substance. Tertullus was more interested in making a favorable impression on Felix than he was in conveying the truth. Reading the speech of Tertullus, one would think that Felix was a peacemaker and benefactor of the Jews. However, the facts would not have backed up that conclusion. Felix had a reputation for being cruel and treacherous.

Three charges were made against Paul:

- He was a troublemaker, stirring up riots among the Jews all over the world.
- He was the ringleader of the Nazarene sect.
- He desecrated the Temple in Jerusalem.

The first charge was serious, because it involved cities throughout the Roman Empire where Paul had preached. Inquiry of Roman authorities in these cities would prove this allegation to be false and prove that the Jews were the ones responsible for stirring the people to riot, not Paul. The charge could not stand up to an impartial investigation.

The second charge was interesting. Tertullus called Paul a "Nazarene." Jews refused to call Jesus' followers "Christians," because the name was derived from "Christ," which means "the Messiah." They rejected Jesus as the promised Messiah of God, so they would naturally refuse to honor His followers with such a moniker. Instead, Tertullus used the derogatory term "Nazarene" and called the followers of Jesus a "sect." The term "sect" implied that Paul was promoting division and heresy among the Jews.

The last charge concerned the desecration or disrespect of the Temple. It was true that Paul was in the Temple when he was savagely attacked, but far from violating its sacredness, he was there to fulfill a solemn Jewish vow. The lies against Paul were woven to give the cloak of respectability to the charges against him and were further enhanced by the presence of the high priest. They were fashioned to deceive Felix and destroy Paul.

Tertullus gave a speech that both flattered Felix and insulted Paul. Neither sort of speech is appropriate for a follower of God. Both of these verbal weapons are demeaning and destructive with the intention of producing personal gain through the use of half-truths. Compliments are different than flattery, and critiques are different than insults. In each case, the former uses the truth to edify and affirm, while the latter uses half-truths to destroy and manipulate.

MEMORY CHALLENGE

1 John 1:7

If we walk in the light, as he is in the light, we have fellowship with one another, and the blood of Jesus, his Son, purifies us from all sin.

4. What derogatory statement was made about Jesus in John 1:45-46?

5. Paul was called a Nazarene. Who else was called a Nazarene in Matthew 2:23?

6. Read John 7:37-43. What was one of the reasons people were perplexed that Jesus came from Nazareth in Galilee?

7. Read Psalm 52:1-7. What does David say about people like Tertullus and the high priest? Describe their language and what they love.

8. Revelation 22:12-15 describes the New Jerusalem. Make a list of those who will not be permitted to go into that city.

9. Using our mouths to speak half-truths, to spread falsehoods, and to deceive is wrong. Paul instructs the Christians in Ephesus to live by a higher standard. What instruction did he give in Ephesians 4:25?

10. How do flattery and insults relate to the ninth commandment, *You shall not give false testimony against your neighbor* (Deuteronomy 5:20)?

DAY TWO

Conscience and Hope

Read Acts 24:10-22.

1. Paul had an opportunity to present his defense to Governor Felix. What was his defense to the charge of stirring up riots?

   What was his defense to being a ringleader of the Nazarene sect?

   What was his defense to desecrating the Temple?

   What reason did he give for being in Jerusalem?

2. With what was Felix familiar?

Paul admitted to worshiping God as a follower of the Way. He denied that his loyalty to Jesus had caused him to abandon the law or the teaching of the prophets. Paul remained true to them both. His hope motivated him to keep his conscience clear before both God and humanity. However, his hope was in God, not in the keeping of the law.

3. Read Hebrews 9:6-10. What is unable to clear the conscience of the worshiper?

   How long were these regulations to be in effect?

4. Read Hebrews 9:14. What is able to cleanse our conscience?

From what is it cleansed?

What does this cleaning enable us to do?

5. In 1 Timothy 4:2, how does Paul describe what happens to the conscience of a liar?

6. In Hebrews 13:18, what is associated with having a clear conscience?

Paul once again takes a clear stand against the Sadducees. He states that he believes in the resurrection of the dead: both the righteous and the wicked. This belief led to his striving always to keep his conscience clear before both God and man. If there is no resurrection, no life after death, then it would be easy to agree with the assertions stated in the Book of Ecclesiastes that life is meaningless. If there is no final judgment, then the unrepentant murderer is no worse off than the faithful and diligent wife and mother. If there is no resurrection, then it would seem that a conscience is a nuisance rather than a guide.

The anticipation of judgment is not the sole motivation for behavior, but it certainly does affect behavior. At the beginning of the semester in an upper-division university class that I taught, I informed the students of when assignments were due and when the tests were to be given. I also informed them that I did not take attendance. On any given day, 30-40 percent of the students would be absent. (I am sure the percentage would be greater if I did not have surprise in-class assignments.) However, on test days I have near perfect attendance. "Judgment day" changes behavior. Driving habits change when a policeman is parked alongside the road. Athletic practices change when the coach walks in the door. The soldiers stand to attention when the general walks down the hall. Judgment affects behavior. And Paul said that his hope in the resurrection, when the wicked and the righteous would stand before God, spurred him on to live in such a way that kept his conscience clear.

7. What does Paul mean in 1 Corinthians 15:19?

8. Who is the source of our hope? (See 1 Timothy 1:1.)

9. What is the basis of the things for which we hope? (See Hebrews 11:1.)

10. What does 1 Peter 3:15-16 say concerning hope?

What is the reason for *your* hope?

MEMORY CHALLENGE

What purifies us from all sin?

DAY THREE

Choices and Convenience

Read Acts 24:22-26.

1. When did governor Felix say he would decide Paul's case?

2. Is there any evidence that Felix tried to contact Lysias the commander or that the commander ever visited Caesarea?

Paul asked Felix to have his accusers name the crime for which he was guilty. Paul repeated for him the words he had shouted in the Sanhedrin. That was all the governor needed to hear. He abruptly concluded the session by saying that he would delay his judgment until he had a chance to talk to Lysias. Until then, Paul would remain in custody with ample freedom to see his friends and receive help from them.

During the days that followed, Felix talked with Paul many times. He had mixed motives for doing this. One motive was money. He hoped Paul would offer a bribe for his release. Maybe he thought Paul still had access to the money he brought from the brothers in Acacia and Macedonia. However, he misjudged Paul's character. Paul was determined to do God's will in God's way and to wait for God's time.

The second reason Felix talked with Paul was curiosity. Felix was interested in what Paul had to say. On one occasion he brought his wife, Drusilla, to hear Paul's teachings. Felix was frightened by what he heard but was not willing to make a decision about Paul or about his teachings concerning Jesus. Felix said he would consider the issue again when it was more convenient.

My daughter has inherited a bad trait from her dad. When asked to clean up, put something away, or do a chore, she often says she will do it "in just a minute," after she finishes what she is doing. When asked to take out the garbage, I often reply by saying, "I'll get to it in just a minute." The timing never seems to be convenient. My daughter and I both need to learn that being obedient and fulfilling one's responsibilities is not a matter of convenience. Important matters should not be postponed simply because they are inconvenient, particularly matters that have eternal consequences. Governor Felix was in dangerous territory.

3. Read Romans 10:1-4. What did Paul say the Israelites tried to do but could not?

4. Compare Deuteronomy 6:20-25 with Romans 1:16-17; 3:21-26. These passages speak of two different kinds of righteousness. How are they different?

5. Read Philippians 3:7-9. For what did Paul suffer the loss of all things?

6. According to 2 Corinthians 6:2, when is the acceptable time to receive Jesus Christ as Savior and Lord?

7. Record an aspect of your spiritual journey that you postponed to a more convenient time.

MEMORY CHALLENGE

Draw a picture below that depicts a portion of the Memory Challenge.

DAY FOUR

Favors and Appeals

Read Acts 24:27—25:12.

1. How long did Governor Felix keep Paul imprisoned?

2. Who took over the position of governor?

Felix never made a judgment about Paul's case, and Paul never offered him a bribe. The weeks turned into months and the months into years. Regardless of whether Felix was actually intrigued by what Paul had to say or was motivated by political convenience, he detained Paul for two years. Paul remained in prison through the transfer of power to Festus.

The Jews had a reputation for being difficult to govern. Maybe in an effort to get off on the right foot with this part of his constituency, the new governor traveled to Jerusalem just three days after taking office. Two years had not changed the feelings of the Jerusalem Jews toward Paul. They met with Festus and asked that Paul be brought back to Jerusalem to be tried. Instead, Festus instructed them to come to Caesarea and establish their charges again. After spending over a week with the Jerusalem Jews, Festus returned to Caesarea to begin the trial.

Charges were once again leveled against Paul. Once again he defended his innocence. Festus was inclined to grant a favor to Paul's accusers and send Paul back to Jerusalem. Paul was probably aware of the plot to kill him and knew that a transfer could mean death. He used his rights as a Roman citizen to appeal his case to Caesar. This meant Paul would be transferred to Rome. Usually such an appeal came subsequent to an unjust sentencing. However, Paul used it to avoid the "death sentence" of being transferred to Jerusalem.

God had promised that Paul would testify about Him in Rome. God also promises to accomplish His purposes through us if we are obedient to Him. He often does His work through our own resources. Paul may have thought that God might intervene in some extraordinary way. However, God simply used a resource Paul had from birth, his citizenship. So often we focus on what we do *not* have rather than on what we *do* have.

At a critical time in my life my dad needed to find new employment. God used my dad's long-time love of boats to lead him to apply for and accept a job with a marine company, so we moved to Detroit. Many good things resulted from this move, not the least of which is that my sister and I met our spouses in Detroit. God can use spectacular interventions; but more often, it seems, He uses resources already at our disposal.

3. What was God's promise to Paul in Acts 23:11?

4. What was one of Joseph's interests and skills that elevated him from slave to the second in command in Egypt? (See Genesis 41:15-16.)

5. What did Moses have that God used to convince the Egyptians and Hebrews that God had sent him? (See Exodus 4:1-5.)

6. Mary and Joseph lived in Nazareth. However, God indicated through the prophet Micah that the Christ would come out of Bethlehem. What was it about Joseph that God used to get them to Bethlehem where Jesus was born? (See Luke 2:1-4.)

7. What did Jesus use to teach the disciples a lesson about servanthood? (See John 13:3-5.)

8. When confronted with a huge and hungry crowd, Philip focused on what the disciples did not have. What did he say? (See John 6:7.)

   Jesus focused on (and gave thanks for) what they did have. What were their resources? (See John 6:9-11.)

9. When Peter was confronted by a beggar on his way to the Temple to pray, what did he acknowledge that he did not have? (See Acts 3:4-6.)

   However, Peter chose to focus on what he *did* have. What was that? (See Acts 3:6-7.)

MEMORY CHALLENGE

Write out a corollary to the Memory Challenge that states it in a negative form (for example, "If we walk in darkness . . .").

DAY FIVE

Dead and Alive

Read Acts 25:13-22.

1. How many days did Agrippa and Bernice stay in Caesarea?

2. What reason did Festus give for not handing Paul over to the Jewish leaders? (See Acts 25:20-21.)

Two of the first guests to visit the new governor were King Agrippa and Bernice. Agrippa was a subordinate to Festus in the Roman hierarchy, but he had influence and important connections in Palestine. Festus was Rome's area representative, while King Agrippa was a puppet prince of Rome and also a practicing Jew. Festus was happy to receive the couple. Agrippa could give him valuable advice in Jewish affairs, because he was familiar with their laws and customs.

During the visit, Festus talked to Agrippa about Paul. He probably was not really interested in Paul as a person; he saw him only as a captive Jew. He was totally unaware that Paul was a powerful spokesman for the "King of Kings" and that his writings would continue to influence people almost 2,000 years later. To Festus, Paul was just a complication in his official relationship with Jewish leaders.

Festus summarized the dispute between the Jews and Paul by saying that they had some conflicts over their own religion. The central issue, Festus said, was about a dead man named Jesus, who Paul claimed was alive. And this really is the central issue for all of us. Was Jesus dead, and is He now live? Paul did not deny that Jesus had died. The records confirmed that fact. However, Paul contended that Jesus was now alive. He had met Him on the road to Damascus, and sharing this good news had become the sole focus of his life. Do you believe that Jesus was once dead and is now alive?

3. Who saw Jesus before He ascended into heaven? (See John 20:18-20.)

4. Paul said that Jesus is alive. What do the following verses tell us the resurrection of Jesus means to believers?

   Romans 5:11

   Hebrews 7:24-25

5. What did Peter say about Jesus in Acts 2:32?

   What did Stephen say about Jesus in Acts 7:52-56?

   How did the crowd respond to Stephen's testimony in Acts 7:57-58?

6. How does Paul describe how the preaching of Christ crucified divides people? (See 1 Corinthians 1:23.)

7. How is Jesus described in regard to those who believe? (See Ephesians 2:19-20.)

8. Describe what Jesus means to you.

MEMORY CHALLENGE

Ask a friend to help you recite the verse.

DAY SIX

Justification and Communication

Read Acts 25:23-27.

1. Who was in attendance when Paul gave his defense before King Agrippa?

2. What did Governor Festus hope to get out of this meeting with King Agrippa?

The group who would hear Paul were the politically elite of Caesarea. Included were high-ranking officers and leading men of the city. Festus decided to use the occasion, and his guests, to his advantage. They would have to determine the charges that would be forwarded to Nero with Paul. Festus may have been worried about incurring the displeasure of Nero by having Paul's case referred to Rome. It was a petty case that should have been settled in Paul's favor immediately. Now it would be difficult to explain to his superior the official behavior that provoked this extreme reaction from his prisoner.

King Agrippa and his sister Bernice made their pompous entrance. Agrippa was the last of the Herod family mentioned in the New Testament. Herod the Great was the one of whom the magi asked, "Where is the one who has been born king of the Jews?" He was responsible for the slaughter of all baby boys in Bethlehem (Matthew 2:16-29). Next was Herod Antipas, who beheaded John the Baptist and became the friend of Pilate (Luke 23:7-12). Agrippa I was the grandson of Herod the Great. He grew up in Rome with members of the imperial families and was the only one to have royalty bestowed upon him. He built Caesarea and considered Christians to be insignificant. He killed James the brother of John (Acts 12). Now the last "Herod," Agrippa II, asked to hear Paul.

3. Read Luke 9:9. Herod Antipas confessed to murder. Whom did he kill?

4. Read Acts 12:21-23. How and why did Agrippa I die?

Before Paul spoke, Festus told the crowd why they had come together. He stated his dilemma very clearly: *It is unreasonable to send on a prisoner without specifying the charges against him* (Acts 25:27). This principle of clearly stating the problem is true in all disputes. Often issues become larger when we keep them to ourselves. Often they become magnified in order to justify a person's anger or bitterness. It is foolish to try to justify one's own attitudes without clearly communicating the reason for one's frustration.

5. The Book of Proverbs says several things about foolishness and communication. Look up the following references, and write in your own words what they mean.

   Proverbs 10:18

   Proverbs 14:16

   Proverbs 18:2

   Proverbs 28:26

   Proverbs 29:11

6. What was Jesus' command to those who were in conflict? (See Matthew 5:23-24.)

7. What did Jesus say about integrity and clear communication? (See Matthew 5:37.)

As mentioned in Part 1 of this Bible study of Acts, I once I asked my wife to join me in visiting some married friends who lived about an hour away. I felt that something was wrong, so I did not wait for an invitation. When we arrived, we found out they were planning to separate and that she was leaving on the bus that evening. I went with the husband on a walk and forced him to be specific about his frustrations with his wife. In essence, the entire argument that led to this drastic measure was based on her refusal to get him a glass of orange juice. The issue had escalated because they had not talked about it. The issue did not merit separation—it merited communication. Finding faults can be done by anyone. Initiating truthful and healthy communication is the work of the wise.

MEMORY CHALLENGE

Recite 1 John 1:5-7.

Acts

■ A Study of Acts 26:1—27:8

LESSON 20

DAY ONE

God's Plans

Read Acts 26, focusing on verses 1-11.

1. With what was King Agrippa acquainted?

2. What did Paul describe as the strictest sect of the Jewish faith?

Paul had an incredible opportunity, one he could not have orchestrated himself. He was standing before royalty, the politically elite of the area, high-ranking officers, the leading men of the city, and the leaders of the Jews from Jerusalem. To this audience he was given permission not only to present a defense to the charges brought against him but also to testify to his conversion and faith in Jesus Christ.

Paul began his defense by saying he was a committed Jew. As a boy in Jerusalem, he gained a reputation by receiving the approval of the leaders of the strictest religious sect in Judaism. He was a Pharisee, and the Pharisees placed special emphasis on the promise and truth of the Resurrection. They upheld hope in the Resurrection as a cardinal item of belief. This was their distinctive doctrine and the one that distinguished them from their Jewish brothers. Their belief in resurrection was also the basis of the ongoing controversy between the Sadducees and Pharisees. The Sadducees denied the Resurrection, and their views were dominant, because they controlled many of the seats of influence and the wealth in Israel.

The collective hope of all Jews, both Sadducees and Pharisees, was the coming of the promised Messiah of God. Only Jews fully understood this hope, so very few of the governor's guests would have understood the nuances of Paul's statements. However, Agrippa would have known. He was a practicing Jew and would have understood Paul when he said, *It is because of my hope in what God has promised our fathers that I am on trial today* (verse 6). Agrippa knew it was wrong to hold Paul in custody for simply proclaiming the fulfillment of the Jewish national hope, a hope he had cherished since childhood; but that is what had happened. Paul said Jesus was the promised Messiah and that this was verified by His resurrection from the dead. Jesus was not dead—He is alive.

Paul's passion for telling others of the incredible news about the resurrection of the Christ had taken him to the marketplace, synagogues, and prisons, from Ephesus to Acacia, and from Philippi to Jerusalem. His earlier life had been dominated by his own agenda. Now he was following the leadership of the Holy Spirit. He could never have orchestrated the events. However, God brought together a king, a governor, and the leading people of the area to hear the message of hope.

3. Of what was Paul convinced before he became a follower of Christ? (See Acts 26:9.)

4. Where did Paul's agenda of persecution take him? (See verse 10-11.)

MEMORY CHALLENGE

1 John 1:8

If we claim to be without sin, we deceive ourselves and the truth is not in us.

5. Jesus described the Pharisees and teachers of the law in Matthew 23. List five things He said about them.

6. What did Jesus promise to do for them? (See Matthew 23:34.)

7. God sent His prophets and messengers to the Pharisees, to a slave girl in Philippi, and to a king in Caesarea. He knew and still knows how to accomplish His purposes.

   If you had been Paul, meeting with fellow believers three years earlier on a strategy to get an audience with the governor to share the Good News, what might your plans have been?

   Briefly review the recent chapters we have studied in Acts, and write how God brought about Paul's testimony before the governor.

8. Record a time when you were frustrated because your plans were messed up, later realizing that God had accomplished His purposes.

DAY TWO

Servant and Witness

Read Acts 26:9-18.

1. At what time of day did Paul see the light, and how bright was it?

2. For the third time we get to read about Paul's experience on the road to Damascus. Find and record the other two references in Acts in which Paul's experience with the risen Christ is recorded.

3. The Lord appointed Paul to do what two things for Him?

Paul knew the Jews opposed him because he was a follower of Jesus. He thought it was important for his audience to understand that at one point he also opposed Jesus. He had been convinced that the followers of the Way were a threat to Judaism. Paul had been certain that his persecution of others was justified. His obsession resulted in cruel and aggressive behavior, all in the name of religious fervor.

Those listening must have realized that a drastic change had taken place in Paul's life. The description he gave of his former actions and purpose were just the opposite of his current testimony and allegiance. Those whom he had once persecuted were now his friends, and those who were once his allies now wanted him dead. Paul explained that the dramatic change in his life came as the result of a personal encounter with Jesus Christ. That event had started a relationship that changed his life forever. His conversion did not take away his passion or zeal, but it did change his focus and purified the motivations of his heart.

Paul's transformation produced one of the greatest witnesses to God's grace and one of the most eloquent teachers of the doctrine of God's grace that the world has ever seen. Therefore, it is easy to overlook the first part of God's appointment of Paul and see only his efforts to turn people *from darkness to light, and from the power of Satan to God* (verse 18). God's appointment of Paul to be His witness is fulfilled in very dramatic ways. However, God also appointed him to be His servant. Allegiance and obedience to God always precedes testimony about God. It is through obedience that one comes to experience the grace of God's lordship. One's life, then, becomes a witness of that grace, and words are one way through which that witness is expressed. But a testimony without a relationship is lifeless; a testimony that is born out of a passionate relationship is compelling.

4. The Lord commissioned Paul to go to both Jews and Gentiles for a specific purpose. What was it? (See Acts 26:18.)

5. What promise did the Lord give Paul to encourage, strengthen, and help him walk with confidence? (See Acts 26:17.)

6. How do you think this promise prepared Paul for what he eventually experienced?

7. Read Luke 22:24-27. What example did Jesus set for His disciples?

8. Paul wrote many letters to believers throughout the world. Some of these letters became books of our Bible. In his opening greetings he often referred to himself as an "apostle." However, in several books he also called himself something else. Read Romans 1:1 and Philippians 1:1. What other way did Paul describe himself?

9. Read Acts 4:18-20. Peter and John speak of both being a servant and being a witness. What phrase speaks of being a servant of God (obedience)?

   What phrase speaks of being a witness for God?

MEMORY CHALLENGE

Write the Memory Challenge on your calendar as a reminder of its importance.

DAY THREE

In God's Hands

Read Acts 26:19-24.

1. When Paul met Jesus, he realized his sin and committed himself to be both a servant and a witness. He was not disobedient to the vision from heaven. From then on, what was the message Paul preached to others?

2. What did Paul say would be the evidence that someone had truly repented?

3. What was the response of Festus to Paul's defense?

Personal testimony is empowered by the Holy Spirit. Whenever we tell others of what Jesus has done for us, as Paul did, we can be assured that the Lord takes our words, protects them, and applies them to the hearts of those who listen.

We are responsible to tell what the Lord has done for us. The Holy Spirit accepts the responsibility of convincing those to whom we speak and those with whom we share life's journey. It is His job, and we are to trust Him. Sometimes trusting Him with the results is difficult, because we want to see them immediately. However, seeing does not require trust. The Father often teaches His children trust and obedience at the same time.

Paul trusted the Holy Spirit to do what he could not do. He certainly remembered how he had opposed Jesus and the testimony of Stephen. Paul disagreed with everything Stephen said, but it did not change the truth of Stephen's words. Sometime later, the Spirit took the truth and brought it to life in Paul's heart. Now Paul had an opportunity to witness to Festus, Agrippa, and the other leaders. He knew the Lord would guide his words and apply them effectively. Paul simply needed to be obedient.

Recently at a conference a gentleman with whom I had spoken at many similar conferences approached me and initiated a conversation. I had seen him at least once a year for the last several years. On this occasion he thanked me for the timeliness of a note I had sent him several months earlier. As he talked, I struggled to remember any such note, much less what I might have said. I simply smiled and listened. Inwardly I thanked God that maybe in this one instance I had simply been obedient to write a note and had actually trusted God with the results. Either that, or this man had me confused with someone else! Regardless, I was reminded how important it is to be obedient and then simply to trust God with the results.

4. Read 2 Timothy 1:8-12.

   Of what should we not be ashamed?

   Why has God saved us?

   When did God first initiate His grace toward us?

   What is God able to guard for us?

5. In 1 Corinthians 3:5-11, Paul talks about the different roles that we might play in fulfilling God's purposes.

   What are Paul and Apollos?

   What was Paul's role with the Corinthians?

What was Apollos's role?

What was God's role?

What is the foundation on which we all build?

6. Write Proverbs 3:5-6 in your own words.

7. In what areas of your life is it difficult to trust God with the results?

MEMORY CHALLENGE

Review some of those things God has forgiven in your life (both actions and attitudes) and those things from which He has saved you.

DAY FOUR

Repentance

Read Acts 26:24-27.

1. What do you think Paul said that made Festus declare that he was insane?

2. How did Paul describe his own words?

3. Who in the audience did Paul say was familiar with what he was saying?

4. Who in the audience was Paul convinced believed in the prophets?

Paul preached a message of repentance and turning back to God. It was not a popular message—then or now. It is an especially difficult message for those who are convinced of their own righteousness. Those who are moving away from God must turn back, or they will perish by going the wrong direction. I am told by a friend who is a pilot that it is possible when flying in a fog to become so disoriented that one could actually be upside down and not realize it. That is why it is so important that a non-instrument-rated pilot not fly in bad weather conditions. Being so disoriented would cause one to pull back on the controls to gain altitude when actually that action would cause the plane to plummet to the ground. In the same way, an incorrect orientation toward God leads to destruction.

After his conversion (his reorientation toward God), Paul made a wonderful discovery. He found that the Scriptures had accurately foretold everything that happened to Jesus. The events of His birth, life, death, and resurrection were in perfect harmony with what the prophets had said. It was a painful realization, because it forced him to acknowledge that Judaism was opposing God. Repentance was necessary and was the path to reconciliation with God.

Festus did not like Paul's words. He was Roman and was not particularly interested in Jewish beliefs or their prophets. But Paul was hoping his message made sense to King Agrippa. He appealed to his knowledge of the prophets.

5. Read 1 Corinthians 2:12-16.

   Why have we received the Spirit, who is from God?

   What happens to the person without the Spirit of God?

   What explanation does this give to the way Fetus responded to Paul's witness?

   How did Paul describe his own mind?

6. Read the following scriptures. Who preached that people should repent?

   Matthew 3:1

   Matthew 4:17

   Mark 6:8-12

   Acts 2:38

   Acts 17:22, 29-30

   Revelation 2:4-5

7. According to Ezekiel 18:30-32, what are the benefits to the person who repents?

8. Is there any area of your life that needs to be "reoriented"? If so, ask God to do so.

MEMORY CHALLENGE

Read the verse that follows the Memory Challenge (1 John 1:9), and thank God for the hope it provides.

DAY FIVE

Almost Persuaded

Read Acts 26:28-32.

1. In what order did the guests leave the assembly hall?

2. What conclusion did the group reach about Paul?

Agrippa squirmed as Paul talked about deeds that were proof of genuine repentance. For Agrippa to repent and turn to God would mean a radical change in lifestyle. Paul understood. It had meant the same thing for him.

Agrippa asked Paul, *Do you think that in such a short time you can persuade me to be a Christian?* (verse 28). The question hints that while Paul was speaking, Agrippa considered it. This was not the first time he had thought about Jesus. He was certainly aware of Jesus' death and the reports of His resurrection. In addition, he was likely familiar with the miraculous healings and bizarre prison experiences of many of the followers of Jesus. Maybe the most curious thing of all was the persistent optimism and hope expressed by these disciples in the face of opposition and persecution.

Paul's testimony added to the mounting body of evidence that proved Jesus was alive. If it was true, then Jesus was the Messiah the prophets had foretold. Probably Agrippa was finding it more difficult to maintain a neutral position about Jesus of Nazareth.

Paul replied to Agrippa's question. He wanted Agrippa to choose to believe in Jesus and to know the reality of His presence and Spirit. Paul wanted the king to know about forgiveness of sins, of peace and joy; but Agrippa had to choose for himself. Instead, Agrippa stood to his feet and left the room, *almost* persuaded to be a Christian. The meeting ended abruptly.

3. What words of Agrippa indicated that he thought Festus should have freed Paul immediately (before he appealed to Caesar)?

4. Based on Acts 25:3-9, was Festus concerned with justice as far as Paul was concerned? Explain.

5. Do we have an indication that anyone who heard Paul speak before Agrippa responded to Jesus in faith?

6. Jesus wept when the people of Jerusalem refused to believe He was the Messiah of God. Read Luke 19:41-44.

   What did the people fail to do?

   Was this also true of those who listened to Paul?

7. Is there any truth from yesterday's lesson that gives us hope concerning those who are *almost* persuaded?

MEMORY CHALLENGE

Recite the verse from memory three to five times.

DAY SIX

Off to Rome

Read Acts 27, focusing on verses 1-8.

1. Why was Paul sailing to Italy? (See Acts 23:11; 25:25.)

2. Based on the pronouns used, who accompanied Paul on this trip?

Festus put a centurion in charge of getting Paul and the other prisoners to Rome. His name was Julius. He secured passage on a ship sailing from Adamyttium, a harbor on the west coast of Asia Minor.

Paul and the others sailed north along the coast of Syria and arrived the next day in the port of Sidon. While there, the commander allowed Paul to stay with friends who ministered to his needs. He returned to the ship refreshed in body and renewed in spirit.

3. Paul received the hospitality of friends in Sidon. Read Romans 12:13 and 16:23. What do these verses tell about Paul's thought on hospitality?

4. Read Hebrews 13:1-2. What do these verses tell us to do?

Their next stop was Myra, the southernmost port in Asia Minor. The usual route would take ships south and west of Cyprus; however, strong winds pushed them north and east of the island.

Time and weather were becoming critical factors in reaching Rome. The approaching winter would soon make sailing the open seas perilous for both the cargo and for the lives of the passengers.

At Myra, the commander found an Egyptian vessel that had a cargo of wheat going to Italy, so he obtained passage for his soldiers and prisoners. By this time it was late September or early October, and winds from the north would soon make sailing impossible. Already the erratic winds prevented the crew from holding the ship on course.

5. Read Romans 8:31-37. These words reflect the thoughts that were fixed in Paul's mind and heart and strengthened him. Which of the statements reflect your greatest need at this time in your life?

6. The love of God is gentle yet tenacious. His love is greater than anything we might face, and nothing can separate us from His love. Spend a few moments and meditate on the incredible love that your Creator has toward you.

MEMORY CHALLENGE

Recite 1 John 1:6-8.

Wisdom of the Word **Bible Study Series**

Acts

■ A Study of Acts 27—28

LESSON 21

DAY ONE

Gentle South Breezes

Read Acts 27, focusing on verses 9-20.

1. What was wrong with the harbor of Fair Havens?

2. Where did the majority want to winter?

3. What encouraged them to lift up the anchors and begin sailing along the shore of Crete?

By the time the ship in which Paul was being transported reached Fair Havens, on the island of Crete, Yom Kippur (the Day of Atonement) had already passed. This meant that it was late September or early October. The seasonal wind shifts were making it increasingly difficult to navigate their northwest journey to Rome. They needed to find an appropriate place to spend the winter, and the Fair Havens harbor was not suitable to the pilot and owner of the ship. They felt the need to get farther up the coast of Crete to the port of Phoenix. When a gentle south wind began to blow, they seized the opportunity and set sail. However, before they reached Phoenix, the winds changed direction, and a violent storm with hurricane force, called the "northeaster," descended on the ship and made navigation almost impossible.

The ship's crew was consumed with saving the ship and thus saving themselves. They allowed the ship to be driven southwest by the winds. When they raised and secured the lifeboat, they passed ropes underneath the boat and tightened them to hold the boat together. Then they lowered the anchors to slow the ship so that if they hit a sandbar, the boat would not be crushed by the force. In desperation they threw cargo and tackle overboard so that the boat would not sit so low in the water. The storm continued unabated for days. Neither the sun nor the stars could be seen, so the sailors had no sense of direction or location. This was not a small boat but rather was large enough to carry 276 people. And yet the winds and seas were so overpowering to the ship that the crew and passengers gave up hope of surviving.

Many of us have made a decision, accepted an assignment, initiated a relationship, or embarked on an adventure feeling that a "gentle south breeze" has been the confirmation we needed to proceed. Many of us have also experienced how a gentle south breeze can turn into a violent "northeaster." Sometimes a vocational change during a gentle south breeze turns painful when the northeaster of a company "downsizing" takes place. Often the gentle south breeze of children in grade school can turn into the chaotic northeaster of children working through adolescence. Sometimes the gentle south breeze of a friendship can turn into the emotional fury of misunderstanding and betrayal. Sometimes it is someone else's poor decision or lack of wisdom that creates our perilous circumstances.

The storms of life can hit us with the same suddenness and intensity as a spring tornado in Oklahoma. They

MEMORY CHALLENGE

1 John 1:9

If we confess our sins, he is faithful and just and will forgive us our sins and purify us from all unrighteousness.

can threaten to destroy us and leave us feeling helpless and hopeless. As the stars and sun could not be seen by the sailors, so the storms of life can sometimes cloud our view of those things that typically provide guidance or direction. Maintaining any equilibrium, particularly spiritual equilibrium, seems nearly impossible.

4. Read Luke 8:22-25.

   Where did Jesus say they were going?

   Why did the disciples think they were not going to make it?

   What did Jesus do to the winds and seas?

5. Where had God told Paul he was going to share his testimony? (See Acts 23:11.)

   What reason did Paul have to doubt God's promise?

6. In Genesis 18:14, God asked Abraham a question that is always appropriate to ask when faced with the storms of life. Record the question below.

7. Describe a personal situation in which a gentle south breeze became a disheartening northeaster.

8. How can your answer to question 6 help you with the situation described in question 7?

DAY TWO

Counsel and Intercession

Read Acts 27:21-32.

1. To whom did the angel appear?

2. What was the angel's message?

3. How many nights were they driven cross the Adriatic Sea?

The crew, soldiers, prisoners, and passengers were all discouraged. The storm had sapped their energy, and each passing day had whittled away at their hope of survival. They had not eaten for days, and their instinct to survive had dwindled away. In the midst of these bleak circumstances, God sent an angel. During the night this angel stood by Paul and provided words of encouragement. He reiterated God's promise that Paul would stand before Caesar. In addition, the angel promised that all those aboard the ship would be saved. The next day Paul communicated the words of encouragement to the others.

The winds did not immediately cease. The seas did not immediately grow calm. The clouds did not immediately disappear. There was still no land in sight. And yet Paul entreated them to keep up their courage. He was convinced that God's promises were more dependable than life's circumstances, that God's protection was more powerful than life's storms, that God's plans were more certain than life's problems. However, it is important to remember that Paul was the only one who saw or heard the angel. The others listened to Paul and had to decide on the credibility of his words. To some he was the leader of the Church, but to most he was simply a prisoner.

An elderly woman in our church passed away a few years ago. She did not hold a position of leadership, nor was she influential in church governance. However, she was greatly respected for her spiritual sensitivity and wisdom. My wife had met her many years before we started attending her church. My wife shared with her the details of a physical problem that had hindered the fulfillment of a dream in our family's journey. The problem had created a dark cloud of discouragement. This wonderful woman placed us on her prayer list and interceded for us in prayer over the course of several years. Her prayers and God's provision were greater than our circumstances. A healing took place, and God got us through the storm. I never saw or heard an angel, but I learned to listen to the prayers and godly advice of this woman and of others who have a close walk with the Lord. God often uses the counsel of godly people to guide and encourage us.

4. According to Proverbs 12:15, to what does a wise person listen?

5. Read Psalm 1:1-2. To whose counsel should we not listen?

6. Name a person in your life whose spiritual journey you trust and whose counsel you value.

7. On whose behalf does Paul encourage Timothy to offer intercessory prayer? (See 1 Timothy 2:1.)

8. According to Romans 8:34, who sits at the right hand of God, and what is He doing?

9. In 2 Peter 3:9, the author seems to comment on the very type of circumstances that Paul and his companions faced on the ship. According to the verse, how might God use circumstances like Paul's to fulfill His will?

   Describe a situation in your life that might be addressed by that verse.

MEMORY CHALLENGE

Write an e-mail to yourself that includes the Memory Challenge. Keep it in your in-box for the week, and read it each day.

DAY THREE

Giving Thanks

Read Acts 27:33-39.

1. How many were on board the ship?

2. Where did they decide to run the ship aground?

The storm had been raging for 14 days when the sailors sensed that they were approaching land. They had no idea where they were, but they feared being dashed against the rocks of whatever coastline they were approaching. After taking several soundings, their suspicions were confirmed. The depth of the water was decreasing rapidly. They dropped the anchors from the bow to slow the boat, and they prayed for daylight so that they might see what was ahead.

None of them had eaten for days, so Paul encouraged them all to have something to eat. They would need strength to make it to shore in the morning. He encouraged them again by telling them that no one would lose a single hair from his head. After speaking, Paul took some bread, gave thanks, and ate it. The others were encouraged and ate some bread as well.

Notice that in the midst of severe circumstances, Paul offered thanks for God's provision. Prayers filled with a recitation of difficulties and problems may be given to ask for God's help. And such petitions to God are perfectly appropriate. However, reciting God's provisions instead of life's problems is a powerful spiritual discipline. It focuses attention on God's care and resources, not on our discouraging circumstances. It opens up the mind to the hope of a future based on how God has taken care of one's needs in the past. An attitude of gratitude replaces obstacles with possibilities.

3. When faced with a hungry crowd of 5,000 and having only five loaves and two fish, what did Jesus do? (See John 6:11.)

4. When Jesus offered bread and wine to His disciples at the Passover meal prior to His crucifixion, He used them as symbols of His suffering and sacrificial death on the Cross. Facing the darkest hour of His life, He took these symbols of pain and agony and gave _______________ for them (Matthew 26:26-27).

5. Read 1 Thessalonians 5:16-18.

   What are we told to do?

   When are we to give thanks?

6. When Paul wrote the letter to the Philippians, he had a spirit of gratitude. What did he say in the first three verses of that letter that reveals his gratefulness to God?

7. According to Psalm 100:4, how should we enter into God's presence?

8. According to Romans 1:21, what happened to the people who were characterized as neither glorifying God nor giving thanks to Him?

9. Just as negative thinking can be contagious, so gratitude can influence people in a positive way. In the Scripture reading for today, what did the other passengers do that indicates Paul's influence on them?

10. Write below some of the words to a song of your choice that speaks of being grateful or thankful.

MEMORY CHALLENGE

What is God's response to our confession of sin?

DAY FOUR

God's Intervention

Read Acts 27:39-44.

1. What prevented the boat from making it to the sandy beach?

2. What broke the boat to pieces?

3. What plan did the soldiers have?

4. Who prevented them from carrying out the plan?

After days of drifting at sea, the sailors finally saw land. The place did not look familiar, but they spotted a welcome sight: a bay with a sandy beach. They guided the ship in the direction of the beach, cut anchors, and allowed the boat to sail. Their hopes soared, but, while still a good distance from shore, the bow stuck fast in the sandbar. The seas were still raging from the storm and the waves began to tear the boat apart. Then the centurion announced his rescue plan. He ordered everyone who could swim to jump overboard and swim to shore. All those who could not swim were to look for a plank of wood that had broken off the disintegrating ship. They were to jump in the water, grab the plank of wood, and float to shore. It was not a very glamorous plan; however, everyone reached the shore safely.

Now when I think of God's intervention, I sometimes hope for an intervention like what Paul experienced when the angel visited him in the night. However, for 275 people on board the ship, there was no such angelic visitation. Nevertheless, God's promise was fulfilled for all of them. I can imagine how skeptical I might have been if I had been one of the companions of Paul who did not know how to swim. I would have been in the water, hanging on to a battered piece of wood, convinced that either the large waves would drown me or my strength would give out and the sea would swallow me. I would have been asking, "Where is God, and why can't He part these waters like He did the Red Sea?"

Many of us look for God in the spectacular, or we limit Him to the way in which we would solve a problem if we had God's powers. However, God often uses the ordinary to bring about His purposes. His intervention often looks like a battered piece of wood, but He can accomplish His purposes through the simple plans of someone like the centurion. Everyone made it to shore, and not a single hair was lost. For those who were looking, God's "fingerprints" could be found on the broken planks from the ship. They can also be found on the many planks of wood that help us to make it through the storms of life. It is easy to miss God's intervention. However, if we look, we will find His fingerprints are all around us.

5. In what form did God choose to enter the world? (See Luke 2:8-12.)

6. Jesus' death (the sacrifice by which we are saved) was done through what common first-century practice? (See Mark 15:27.)

7. List some ways in which God's fingerprints are seen in nature.

8. List some "pieces of wood" that were God's intervention in your life (such as the encouraging words of a friend, the wisdom of a child, the miracle of a bag of groceries, the timing of a letter, an unexpected check, or an inspiriting book).

MEMORY CHALLENGE

Use the Memory Challenge as a basis for a prayer.

DAY FIVE

God's Redemption

Read Acts 28. Focus on verses 1-11.

1. On what island had the men landed?

2. How long did they stay on the island?

The storm system was still causing some rain, and the temperatures had dropped. The weather-beaten travelers gathered together on the beach and were met by the natives of island, who were unusually kind. They welcomed the group and built them a fire. Paul wanted to contribute, so he gathered some wood and placed it onto the fire. In the process a snake struck at Paul, bit his hand, and held on until he could shake it off into the blaze. The islanders assumed that Paul would die from the snakebite, concluding that he was a murderer and that this was his just punishment. However, Paul not only did not die, but his hand did not even swell up. So they changed their minds and concluded that he was a god. Of course, neither conclusion was correct.

An island official invited Paul and his companions to stay with him for three days. When Paul found out that the father of the official was very ill, he visited him, prayed for him, and God brought about his healing. For the next three months the islanders brought Paul and Luke their sick, and they were healed. The stay in Malta was beneficial for the other passengers as well. They received the hospitality of the islanders, found an Alexandrian ship that was heading north, and were given needed supplies for the journey. Our Heavenly Father is a God of redemption. He not only redeems people—He also redeems situations, circumstances, events, and time. The disastrous shipwreck can prove to be a blessing to all.

The people of Malta may not have heard about Jesus for decades had God not used these difficult circumstances to bring about His purposes. God never promised Paul a direct route to Rome, just that he would get there. He allowed the people of Malta to hear the Good News and blessed the travelers with island hospitality during their winter stay. Apparently God is concerned not only with our destination but also with those we meet on the way.

3. Consider how God provided for all the people in this story. List below the ways in which God provided for their needs.

   Publius, the chief official of the island

   The citizens of the island

   Paul

   Paul's traveling companions

   The centurion, the soldiers, and the sailors

4. Describe how God has provided redemption in your life.

5. Describe a time when you experienced unexpected hospitality.

6. Offer a prayer that God would use you to bless someone you encounter today on the way to your "destination."

MEMORY CHALLENGE

During mealtime ask a family member or friend to test you on reciting the Memory Challenge.

DAY SIX

God's Work Continues

Read Acts 28:11-31.

1. Where and with whom did Paul and his companions spend a week before arriving in Rome?

2. Who had heard that Paul was coming, and how far did they travel to meet him?

Paul and the other passengers had boarded an Alexandrian ship in Malta that was heading for Rome. The ship sailed to a coastal town of Italy, where the group disembarked. There they met a group of Christian brothers who offered the travelers their hospitality. The journey to Rome now required a long walk from the coast. They likely traveled the road called the Appian Way.

Others in Italy had heard that Paul was coming. He had written a letter to the people of Rome several years earlier, and it had likely been widely circulated by this time. This letter, the Book of Romans, was filled with wisdom, truth, sound doctrine, and love. In it he had mentioned that he wanted to come for a visit (Romans 15:23-24). However, he certainly did not plan to visit as a prisoner. Regardless, the Christians in Rome were looking forward to his arrival. Some traveled many miles to meet him on the way. Paul was encouraged at the sight of them and was blessed by their kindness and grace. They were members of his spiritual family.

3. When we put our faith in Jesus, we are adopted into God's family. What do the following scriptures tell us about the family of God?

   John 1:12

   Romans 8:15

   2 Corinthians 6:18

Galatians 3:26

Galatians 4:6

4. What were the conditions under which Paul lived as a prisoner? (See Acts 28:30.)

Within three days of Paul's arrival in Rome, he invited Jewish leaders to come to his house. He explained to them why he was in bonds and presented his case in the same way he had done before King Agrippa. The Christian brothers probably knew why Paul was coming to Rome, but the Jewish leaders did not. They had not heard any bad reports about him, only that people were talking against the sect that followed Jesus as the Christ. They listened to Paul's arguments and explanations of the kingdom of God. Some were convinced and believed; others did not.

5. What were Paul's activities in Rome during the last two years of Luke's account?

6. What did Paul use to convince his fellow Jews that Jesus was the Christ? (See verse 23.)

7. Are you committed to study God's Word so the Lord can equip you to tell others of Jesus and His love?

Throughout the Book of Acts, Luke shows us that Jesus was truly a stumbling block to the Jews. Some accepted Him; the majority did not. However, the Good News quickly spread among the Gentiles to the uttermost parts of the earth.

Through the Book of Acts, Luke teaches his friend Theophilus, and the rest of us, how God protects, empowers, and grows His Church. Christ is the bridegroom, and the Church is His bride. Peter and Paul were two of the early leaders of the Church whom Luke used to show God's goodness and grace.

The story ends with Paul physically in chains but spiritually free. He communed with his Creator and ministered to all who came to see him. He preached the kingdom of God boldly and without hindrance. May God allow us to live in that same spiritual freedom.

MEMORY CHALLENGE

Write the Memory Challenge along with the previous verses (1 John 1:5-9).

Notes

Lesson 12, Day 1

1. Adam Clarke, *Adam Clarke's Commentary*, <www.godrules.net/library/clarke>, 1893.

Lesson 12, Day 3

1. Clarke, *Adam Clarke's Commentary.*

Lesson 12, Day 4

1. Clarke, *Adam Clarke's Commentary.*

Lesson 13, Day 5

1. Gerald M. Goldhbaer, *Organizational Communication*, 6th ed. (Boston: McGraw-Hill, 1993).
2. Clarke, *Adam Clarke's Commentary.*

Lesson 14, Day 4

1. Clarke, *Adam Clarke's Commentary.*

Lesson 15, Day 1

1. *Robertson's Word Pictures of the New Testament* (<http://bible.crosswalk.com/commentaries>).

Lesson 15, Day 4

1. Clarke, *Adam Clarke's Commentary.*

Lesson 15, Day 6

1. *Acts: Model for Today's Church* (Nashville: Serendipity House, 2003).

Lesson 17, Day 5

1. Clarke, *Adam Clarke's Commentary.*

Wisdom Notes*

Date ______________________

Book ______________________

Lesson No. ______________________

Scripture Ref. ______________________

*You may make copies of this sheet to use for note taking as you work through the lessons of this Bible study.

God Can!

"Write down clearly on tablets what I reveal to you, so that it can be read at a glance. Put it in writing, because it is not yet time for it to come true. But the time is coming quickly, and what I show you will come true. It may seem slow in coming, but wait for it; it will certainly take place, and it will not be delayed."

Habakkuk 2:2-3 (TEV)

Use this page to keep a dated record of your prayer requests and God's responses to them.

DATE	I ASK GOD	HE ANSWERS	DATE